Mans.

GW00729976

LIVE WIRES

ANGUS & ROBERTSON PUBLISHERS
London • Sydney • Melbourne • Singapore • Manila

First published in the United Kingdom by Angus & Robertson (UK) Ltd, 1982
First published in Australia by Angus & Robertson Publishers, Australia, 1982
Second impression 1982

© Angus McGill & Kenneth Thomson 1982
National Library of Australia
Cataloguing-in-publication data.

McGill, Angus
    Live wires.
    ISBN 0 207 14159 2.
    1. Telegraph. I. Thomson, Kenneth. II. Title.
384.1'4

Typeset in 11 pt Stymie by Setrite Typesetters
Printed in Great Britain

LIVE WIRES

ANGUS McGILL with KENNETH THOMSON

ANGUS & ROBERTSON PUBLISHERS

CONTENTS

IN THE BEGINNING...

Sometimes you must address an aunt in a hurry. Sometimes you must declare war. Sometimes you must say 'Congratulations stop may all your troubles be little ones stop'.

Runners did it well for a while. They padded along jungle paths with your message in a cleft stick to everyone's satisfaction. When the awful Pizarro landed in Peru in 1533 it took less than twelve hours for a message to reach the Only Inca in his capital city two hundred miles away.

Smoke signals were good too and so were beacons. You had these beacons on hilltops and when, say, the Armada hove into view, you lit them one after another. The news would reach Carlisle in no time.

Or there were pigeons, used by the Romans, the Rothschilds and, for a while, by *The Times,* flapping reliably across country with messages in silk purses tucked under their wings.

Then there were good modern inventions like the heliograph, invented by the Moors in the eleventh century and a sensation at the time. Using a small mirror the heliograph flashed the sun's rays to a distant point where someone was waiting with the code. One flash for 'hello' and two for 'love from Mum, Dad and all at No. 5'; there was no end to what you could say on the heliograph as long as the sun was out.

IN THE BEGINNING...

Ah yes, as long as the sun was out. This proviso did prove rather a drawback in Great Britain, where the heliograph made little impression. The new Speaking Trumpet, however, could be used on the dullest day. You shouted into it and persons some way off sometimes got the gist, particularly if equipped with the new Ear Trumpet, another good idea.

In 1668 these devices seemed to have a future but alas they too were overtaken by progress. By the late eighteenth century all the talk was of the astounding new semaphore which the French were using to connect Paris with their frontier armies; devilish clever, all agreed.

The British Admiralty moved fast. Within fifty years their Lordships had established a line of semaphore towers between London and Portsmouth, a wonder of the day. With a great clatter of shutters messages simply flew from tower to tower. It didn't work in fog, of course. Still, in the whole of 1839 the weather interrupted the system on only twenty-nine days, so that was all right and, taking one thing with another, the Admiralty was well pleased with its investment.

The semaphore line didn't last long, all the same. Within a few years a new and totally revolutionary system was to bring these proud towers tumbling down and sweep all competitors aside.

The Electric Telegraph was on its way.

People had known about electricity for fully a hundred years but no one could think what to do with it.

Scientists did experiments. Benjamin Franklin flew his kite in that thunderstorm and discovered weather and in 1743 the Abbé Nollet wired a number of Carthusian monks together and gave them a simultaneous electric shock. You could see it was simultaneous by the way they all jumped at the same time. But apart from that what good was it?

Then it began to occur to people that you might be able to use it to send messages. From then on, all over Europe and indeed America too, persons of a scientific bent spent hours with lengths of wire and pith balls suspended on silk, with zinc plates and cups of mercury, with magnets and sheets of blotting paper, trying to work out how.

William Fothergill Cooke and Charles Wheatstone got there first; or anyway they got to the patent office first which is sometimes better.

Cooke was a gifted amateur, Wheatstone was Professor of Experimental Philosophy at King's College, London, and inventor, what's more, of the concertina. Before long they couldn't stand the sight of each other but what of that? Apart they had been working on telegraphs of their own and hitting snags. Together they produced one that actually worked and in 1837 took out their historic patent for 'Improvements in Giving Signals and Sounding Alarums in Distant Places by means of Electric Currents transmitted through Metallic Circuits'.

But who needed such a thing? And who could afford one? Giving signals and sounding alarums in distant places was clearly going to be an expensive business.

Luckily the perfect clients were right at hand: the railway companies. They urgently needed something better than a whistle to stop their fine new trains,

IN THE BEGINNING...

chuffing along the brand new single tracks, from meeting head-on and, of course, they were as rich as you could please.

So in July 1837 the first Wheatstone and Cooke electric telegraph was rigged up between the railway stations at Euston and Camden Town for a demonstration in front of the directors of the London and Birmingham railway. The instrument they used was the Wheatstone four-needle telegraph, which could send as many as five words a minute as long as the words were short.

The directors were grave and potent men and among them stood the great engineer, Robert Stephenson. He watched and listened and, while Cooke at one end and Wheatstone at the other held their breath, sent his verdict clicking down the line.

It was the first true telegram to be sent anywhere in the world and it was everything a telegram should be — dramatic, memorable and economical, giving the maximum information in the minimum number of words.

BRAVO telegraphed Mr Stephenson.

Stephenson wanted to run the new telegraph all the way along the new railway line he was building to Liverpool but the other directors wouldn't have it. It was such an expense and wasn't it very complicated, all those wires? New-fangled was what it was in their opinion and Stephenson could not deny it.

Happily, another great engineer had seen the test too: the dashing Isambard Kingdom Brunel of the Great Western Railway. And his directors always listened to *him.* So it was that the world's first practical electric telegraph went into daily use in July 1839 on the stretch of line between Paddington and West Drayton. West Drayton, or so it is believed, had never made history before.

The Americans, I am sorry to report, were rather behind in this matter though they nearly got in first. Their Mr Morse appears to have had his electric telegraph ready in 1836 but no one would take him seriously. He was a portrait painter after all, not an electrician. 'Stick to your last,' they said; but he wouldn't and, in the end, Congress stumped up $30,000 for a line between Washington and Baltimore. It took two years to build but at last, in 1844, the first American telegraph was ready and Mr Morse was ready to send the first American telegram.

He had had some years to think up a good one and now he was ready for posterity.

WHAT HATH GOD WROUGHT? telegraphed Mr Morse.

While some tried to answer this interesting question others got on with the job in hand. There were, after all, fortunes to be made, a whole continent to equip, a coast to be linked with a coast and, in the manner of the times, desperate companies ready to compete ferociously for a piece of the action.

From then on the electric telegraph raced away. Telegraph lines followed railway lines wherever they went, first in iron tubes, then slung high on the new telegraph poles. In towns they were strung across the rooftops, wrapped around chimney pots, looped from parapet to gable end. In the country they went from tree to tree and soon Europe and America were covered in a spider's web of copper wire.

IN THE BEGINNING...

The police were quickly interested. On 28 August 1844 telegrams sent from Paddington to Slough led to the arrest of Oliver Martin and Fiddler Dick, who were picking pockets in the third compartment of the first second-class carriage.

A few months later they caught a bigger fish. John Tawell, having murdered his mistress, caught the train to London. The ticket clerk telegraphed the police at Paddington:

A MURDER HAS JUST BEEN COMMITTED AT SALT HILL AND THE SUSPECTED MURDERER WAS SEEN TO TAKE A FIRST CLASS TICKET FOR LONDON BY THE TRAIN WHICH LEFT SLOUGH AT 7H 42M PM. HE IS IN THE GARB OF A QUAKER WITH A BROWN GREAT COAT WHICH REACHES NEARLY DOWN TO HIS FEET. HE IS IN THE LAST COMPARTMENT OF THE SECOND FIRST-CLASS CARRIAGE...

The police were waiting when Tawell got off the train. They followed him to Islington, arrested him and he was subsequently hanged. It was hard luck on Tawell but good publicity for the electric telegraph.

Newspapers were quick off the mark too. At first *The Times* rather sniffily printed 'Telegraphic Rumours' but in time it was printing Mr Reuter's telegrams like everyone else.

The Times' readers took up their customarily passionate positions. What concerned them was the etymological purity of the new word. Should it be 'telegram' or 'telegrapheme'?

To the fury of the purists, 'telegram' won and to the pleasure of all except perhaps Fiddler Dick its numbers increased and multiplied. Professor Wheatstone's apparatus grew ever more sophisticated and was soon providing a whole new field of employment for nice young ladies of the lower-middle classes. The companies required them to be unmarried and between the ages of eighteen and thirty and to work ten hours a day for six days a week under the strict supervision of a matron. The jobs were much sought after.

Telegraph companies multiplied too. In the first twenty years sixty-four were formed. Most went under before long but the big ones, Electric & International and the Magnetic, were doing well enough. Imagine, then, their dismay when they heard what Mr Disraeli had in mind for them. Nationalisation, no less!

They were shocked. They complained. They took their case to the top. But generous terms from the marauding government made them see things in a better light and in 1868 the telegraph, which had been the first practical use to be made of electricity, now became the first private enterprise to become state-owned.

Of course, there were critics, prophets of doom who said it would never again make a profit and they were right enough. The telegraph service never did make money for the state and it is said that its financial failure stopped successive governments nationalising anything else for fifty years.

The telegraph was indispensable in no time. Marshall McLuhan now says that it

IN THE BEGINNING...

was a major trauma and that it ushered in the 'Age of Anxiety and Pervasive Dread'. And perhaps it did, but people were far too busy sending telegrams to notice.

Furthermore the nation discovered a new appetite for news and the telegraph obligingly filled it. When, for instance, the Prince of Wales fell ill in 1871 the news was flashed to the furthest corners of the land and a poet, some say Alfred Austin, one day to be Poet Laureate, wrote his famous lines:

Across the wires the electric message came:
'He is no better, he is much the same.'

The Viceroy of India testily complained that all this instant communication was sapping the morale of his district officers while Lord Beaconsfield, dealing as best he might with the Eastern Question, found Queen Victoria watching his every move. 'Her Majesty,' he confided to a friend, 'writes every day and telegraphs every hour.'

Meanwhile controversy raged. Was 'alright' one word or two? Was 'mother-in-law' one word or three? Why should South Kensington count as two words while South Shields counted as one?

In the House of Commons Sir Mancherjee Bhownaggree had a question for the Postmaster General. Would he issue instructions that in future Charing Cross and Bethnal Green should each count as only one word? 'No Sir,' said the Postmaster General.

America had its own problems. Posses in the West were cutting the cables to lynch criminals and others, a plain misuse of company property. And in the Australian outback two cablemen were speared to death by Warramunga tribesmen and Aborigines were constantly pinching insulators to use as axe-heads. Still the cable layers soldiered on there and in two years had finished an overland cable, three thousand kilometres long on 36,000 telegraph poles and with a new town, Alice Springs, named after the wife of the chief engineer, bang in the middle.

Back in England the British Post Office allowed no one to make axe-heads of its insulators or in any other way interrupt its service which was rightly considered a miracle of the age. Even those who sent hoax telegrams, such as REPORT ROYAL NAVAL BARRACKS DEVONPORT FORTHWITH were pursued by the full majesty of the law and thoroughly told off when caught. The British Post Office did not care for jokes.

What they did care for was accuracy and speed; above all speed. Miles of pneumatic tubing was installed under city streets so that telegrams zipped backwards and forwards underfoot night and day and platoons of smart lads were recruited for instant telegram delivery. They were put into uniforms, issued with bicycles and paraded for inspection first thing every morning.

The world got steadily smaller as the telegraph spread wider. In 1851, at their second attempt, the brothers Brett succeeded in laying a cable under the English Channel from Dover to Cape Gris-Nez and the news was rushed to Queen Victoria who was just closing the Great Exhibition. She loved to be the first to know.

IN THE BEGINNING...

After that it was only a matter of time before cables were being laid under every strait, every sea, every ocean. In 1866 a cable stretched from one side of the Atlantic to the other, an astounding achievement. Six years later London was in telegraphic contact with Australia.

As if all this was not enough, the amazing new invention of wireless telegraphy ended the isolation even of ships at sea as Dr Crippen was to discover to his cost. There was now nowhere you could hide from the electric telegraph.

It was the golden age of telegraphy. By 1895 more than seventy-eight million telegrams a year were being dealt with in the United Kingdom alone. No other country took to the telegram as keenly as it did.

Alas, it did not last long. Alexander Graham Bell invented the telephone and, slowly at first, then more quickly, then at a gallop, the telegram went into a decline.

It has been in a decline for fifty years now and the process continues. The pneumatic tubes have gone, the telegram boys have gone, even the yellow envelopes are going. Numbers dwindle, costs soar and every telegram sent costs the poor Post Office money and there are some who actually say that the whole service should be scrapped.

What outrage is this? It is as well Sir Charles Wheatstone did not live to see this day, not to mention Sir William Fothergill Cooke. They would have had a thing or two to say.

The telephone is all right, of course, very useful and all that. But to lose the telegram! It is unthinkable and I would thank governments not to think it.

The telegram is irreplaceable and that is the truth. No other form of communication is so urgent. None brings with it such a sense of occasion or arrives with such impact. No other is so blissfully *short.*

Short: that is the heart of the matter, shortness is the telegram's greatest quality. People write too much. We drown in words. The situation gets more serious by the hour and I'm as bad as anyone. I see what I must do though. I must send a telegram.

THE TELEGRAM GOES TO WAR

The taking of Fort Sumter in Charleston Harbour in April 1861 was the first military engagement of the American Civil War. It was also the first appearance of the electric telegraph on the battlefield. It did most gallantly as all agreed.

The fort was being held by forces of the north, commanded by Major Robert Anderson. It was being attacked by the forces of the south, commanded by General Pierre Beauregard, with Mr L.P. Walker, the south's Secretary of War, over the way in Charleston.

It was a properly gentlemanly affair, as the exchange of telegrams between the two sides makes clear. And as telegraphese had not yet been invented the telegrams were delivered hand-written in English, commas, full stops and all.

General Beauregard to L.P. Walker, Secretary of War, Charleston:

AN AUTHORISED MESSENGER FROM PRESIDENT LINCOLN HAS JUST INFORMED GENERAL PICKENS AND MYSELF THAT SEVERAL HAMPERS OF CANVAS-BACK DUCKS, WILD TURKEYS, CORN CAKES, AND MATERIALS FOR BRANDY-SMASHES AND COCK-TAILS WILL BE SENT TO FORT SUMTER PEACEABLY OR OTHERWISE.

L.P. Walker, Secretary of War, to General Beauregard, Montgomery:
STOP 'EM. KEEP WHAT YOU LIKE AND SEND THE REST TO ME. GIVE
MAJOR ANDERSON NOTICE TO QUIT. IF THAT WON'T DO PUT YOUR MEN IN
POSSESSION.

General Beauregard to L.P. Walker, Secretary of War, Charleston:
DEMAND SENT AT 12. ALLOWED TILL 6 O'CLOCK FOR DINNER.

L.P. Walker, Secretary of War, to General Beauregard, Montgomery:
TELEGRAPH WHAT MAJOR ANDERSON SAYS TO THAT.

General Beauregard to L.P. Walker, Secretary of War, Charleston:
MAJOR ANDERSON REPLIES 'I HAVE THE HONOUR TO ACKNOWLEDGE THE
RECEIPT OF YOUR COMMUNICATION, DEMANDING ME TO EVACUATE THIS
FORT, AND TO DINE BEFORE SIX, WITHOUT WAITING TO RECEIVE
SUPPLIES. I REGRET THAT MY OBLIGATIONS TO MY GOVERNMENT AND
MY OWN DIGESTIVE ORGANS, PREVENT MY COMPLIANCE.' HE ADDS 'I WILL
AWAIT THE FIRST SHOT AND THEN DRINK YOUR GOOD-HEALTH IN A BRANDY
SMASH.'

L.P. Walker, Secretary of War, to General Beauregard, Montgomery:

FIRE AWAY (BUT DON'T HURT ANYBODY), UNLESS MAJOR ANDERSON WILL SEND YOU THE LATCH-KEY OF THE FORT.

General Beauregard to L.P. Walker, Secretary of War, Charleston:

HE WON'T CONSENT. HE'S NOT SUCH A FOOL AS YOU THINK.

The bombardment then began and after forty hours of resistance, Major Anderson hoisted a flag of truce.

General Beauregard to Major Anderson, Gingham Umbrella, Fort Sumter:

I SEE YOUR CONDITION THROUGH MY TELESCOPE. WE HAVE INTERCEPTED YOUR SUPPLIES. GIVE IN LIKE A GOOD FELLOW, AND BRING YOUR GARRISON TO DINNER, AND BEDS AFTERWARDS. NOBODY INJURED, I HOPE?

Major Anderson to General Beauregard, Montgomery:

MAJOR ANDERSON PRESENTS HIS COMPLIMENTS TO GENERAL G.F. BEAUREGARD, AND HAS MUCH PLEASURE IN ACCEPTING HIS KIND INVITATION TO DINNER AND BEDS. AS NO ONE IS HURT MAJOR ANDERSON FEARS HE SHALL PUT GENERAL G.F. BEAUREGARD TO SOME INCONVENIENCE, THE PARTY BEING A LARGE ONE.

There was no holding the galloping telegraph after that and dismayed military men were quick to realise that war would never be the same again. It was no longer a private matter between generals. Now secretaries of war could get their oar in.

'The confounded telegraph has ruined everything,' complained General Simpson, British Commander-in-Chief in the Crimea.

And as tensions rose in the Transvaal and Dr Jameson led his abortive raid, the first thing he did was get his troopers to chop down the telegraph poles across the Veldt.

The Boers got their own back later on by listening in — to good effect — on the British military telegraph line, the world's first recorded wire-tap. General Roberts did not think anyone could stoop so low.

Messages from the beleaguered garrison at Mafeking could not have cheered the Boers much but they thrilled the folks back home. Colonel Baden-Powell set the tone right from the start:

ALL WELL. FOUR HOURS BOMBARDMENT. ONE DOG KILLED.

The others followed suit. Here is Major Baillie, correspondent for the *Morning Post:*

THIS MORNING THE BOERS ATTACKED US. THE RESULT WAS AS USUAL. THERE IS AN ACHING VOID HERE. PASS THE LOAF.

And Lady Sarah Wilson, the dashing young sister of Winston Churchill, in a telegram from Mafeking to Lady Georgina Curzon:

BREAKFAST CONSISTED OF HORSE SAUSAGES; LUNCH, MINCED MULE AND CURRIED LOCUSTS. WELL.

When the siege was almost over there was a terse telegram from Lord Roberts:

RELIEF ON MAY 18TH.

And, on 17 May as it happened, a major and eight troopers, the advance guard of the relief column, rode in.

Baden-Powell cabled the Queen at once:

HAPPY TO REPORT MAFEKING SUCCESSFULLY RELIEVED TODAY. NORTHERN AND SOUTHERN COLUMNS JOINED HANDS ON 15TH. ATTACKED ENEMY YESTERDAY 16TH ENTIRELY DEFEATING THEM WITH LOSS. RELIEVING FORCE MARCHED INTO MAFEKING THIS MORNING AT NINE. RELIEF AND DEFENCE FORCE COMBINED ATTACKED ENEMY LAAGER SHELLED THEM OUT NEARLY CAPTURING SNYMAN AND TOOK LARGE AMOUNT OF AMMUNITION AND STORES. TOWNSPEOPLE AND GARRISON OF MAFEKING HEARTILY GRATEFUL FOR THEIR RELEASE.

The Queen replied:

I AND MY WHOLE EMPIRE GREATLY REJOICE AT THE RELIEF OF MAFEKING
AFTER THE SPLENDID DEFENCE MADE BY YOU THROUGH ALL THESE MONTHS.
I HEARTILY CONGRATULATE YOU AND ALL UNDER YOU, MILITARY AND
CIVIL, BRITISH AND NATIVES, FOR THE HEROISM AND DEVOTION YOU
HAVE SHOWN. V.R. AND I

But the Colonel had the last word:

YOUR MAJESTY'S MOST GRACIOUS MESSAGE AMPLY REPAYS ANYTHING WE
MAY HAVE SUFFERED AND HEARTENS US TO RENEWED EFFORTS TO UPHOLD
THE HONOUR OF OUR QUEEN.

So ended what the manufacturers of the Smith Premier Typewriter Company,
London, called an 'up-to-date siege with all the modern scientific equipment'. Not
only did the Colonel have the telegraph at Mafeking, observed the Smith Premier
Typewriter Company; he also had a Smith Premier typewriter.

The First World War began in a storm of telegrams. Everyone seemed to be telegraphing everyone else.

War was declared at midnight, 14 August 1914. Mobilisation telegrams had already gone out. They were short and dramatic. This one, in the possession of the Imperial War Museum, is typical. It went to Lieuteuant J.B. Gawthorpe of Leeds:

MOBILIZATION ORDERED JOIN 10 AM FIFTH. COMMANDING.

And, showing just how serious matters were, this telegram was handed in at Exford at 12.20 on that fateful 4 August:

To Rumwell Hall, Taunton:

NO HUNTING IF ENGLAND DECLARES WAR. TUCKER, HUNTSMAN

Well, England did and there wasn't and for four years telegrams brought news of death and despair:

DEEPLY REGRET TO INFORM YOU...
LORD KITCHENER EXPRESSES HIS SYMPATHY...

Then at last there was good news. This telegram for instance, also held by the Imperial War Museum, went out from the headquarters of the 57th Division to the Second Fifth Battalion, the King's Own Royal Lancaster Regiment:

FOLLOWING RECEIVED FROM 5TH ARMY AAA BEGINS AAA HOSTILITIES WILL CEASE AT 1100 HOURS TODAY NOV 11TH AAA TROOPS WILL STAND FAST ON POSITIONS REACHED AT HOUR NAMED AAA LINE OF OUTPOSTS WILL BE ESTABLISHED AND REPORTED TO ARMY HQ AAA REMAINDER OF TROOPS WILL BE COLLECTED AND ORGANISED READY TO MEET ANY DEMANDS AAA ALL MILITARY PRECAUTIONS WILL BE PRESERVED AND THERE WILL BE NO COMMUNICATIONS WITH THE ENEMY AAA FURTHER INSTRUCTIONS WILL BE ISSUED AAA ENDS AAA

The Second World War also began with telegrams of all degrees, telegrams like these:

Noël Coward to his business manager, Jack Wilson:

GRAVE POSSIBILITY WAR WITHIN FEW WEEKS OR DAYS IF THIS HAPPENS
POSTPONEMENT REVUE INEVITABLE AND ANNIHILATION OF ALL OF US
PROBABLE.

Commander-in-Chief Rosyth to all watching W/T stations:

PASS THE FOLLOWING TO ALL BRITISH VESSELS WITH WHICH YOU MAY BE
IN TOUCH DURING THE NEXT 24 HOURS. WAR HAS BROKEN OUT WITH
GERMANY. YOU MUST NOT REPEAT NOT REPEAT NOT GO INTO GERMAN
PORTS.

Timed: 1210/3/9/39

Commander-in-Chief, Portsmouth, 3 September 1939 to 'All concerned at Home
and Abroad from Admiralty':

COMMENCE HOSTILITIES AT ONCE WITH GERMANY.

From Admiralty, 3 September 1939:

WINSTON IS BACK.

From Admiralty, 3 September 1939:

IMMEDIATE. SPECIAL TELEGRAM. <u>TOTAL</u> GERMANY.

And when this war, too, came to an end, this is how some heard the news:

Commander-in-Chief, Fifth Fleet to Fifth Fleet Pacific:

THE WAR WITH JAPAN WILL END AT 1200 ON 15TH AUGUST. IT IS
LIKELY THAT KAMIKAZES WILL ATTACK THE FLEET AFTER THIS TIME AS
A FINAL FLING. ANY EX-ENEMY AIRCRAFT ATTACKING THE FLEET IS TO
BE SHOT DOWN IN A FRIENDLY MANNER.

IN A WORD...

Possibly the most famous telegram ever sent came from Sir Charles Napier, known to every schoolboy of his day as Conqueror of Sind. Having conquered Sind, he sent his telegram:

PECCAVI

(I have sinned)

A joke! A joke by a general in Latin! There can't be many of those.

Alas, famous though this telegram is, it was not a telegram at all. India did not have the electric telegraph in 1843.

Then there was the subaltern who, like Napier, was moved by his emotion to express himself in Latin. His telegram read:

AMO

(I love)

His girl was bewildered; it reached her as:

AMMO

Thomas Mann's daughter, Erika, branded a public enemy by the Third Reich, had written to the English poet W. H. Auden. He was a stranger to her, but she explained that she needed a British passport so would he marry her? She received in reply:

DELIGHTED

Some Oxford undergraduates who heard that Kipling earned ten shillings for every word he wrote sent him ten shillings and asked for one of his very best words. He sent one:

THANKS

One of the earliest surviving Australian telegrams is a mystery. We have the answer but what on earth was the question? Here, anyway, in its entirety, is the cable received in South Australia on the magnetic telegraph on 15 May 1860.
    The Bishop of Newcastle to the Bishop of Adelaide:

IMPOSSIBLE

Then there is the printers' telegram, sent to a colleague on the occasion of his marriage:

STET

Latin again, and part of every printer's vocabulary: 'let it stand'.

On 6 April 1917 Sarah Bernhardt sent a telegram to her family in France. They opened it with trembling fingers. The divine Sarah was far away in America and seriously ill; they expected the worst. The message they got was a single powerful word:

HURRAH

The 6 April 1917 was the day the United States entered the war.

Bernhardt's most famous telegram was also as brief as it could be. She had never forgiven Germany for the war of 1870. A German promoter sent her a wire: what would it take to get her to appear in Germany? She wired back her terms:

ALSACE-LORRAINE

You could say this about one-word telegrams: they didn't cost much. To many telegram senders, some of them rich, this was a major recommendation.

The great diva Melba hated to waste money on telegrams. Beverley Nichols who was once her secretary says she would spend half an hour trying to delete unnecessary words.

Her favourite device was 'touched thought'. This meant 'I am touched by your thought'. Sometimes, if moved, she would make it 'deeply touched thought' or even, if the person was important enough, 'deeply touched your thought'.

In *Evensong,* his book about her, Beverley Nichols says that a dreadful mishap arose from this practice. A dinner invitation arrived with a large basket of orchids. 'I certainly won't dine with that woman,' said Melba. 'She says I drink. Send her a telegram: "Regret indisposed".'

Nichols reminded her about the orchids. 'You can add "touched thought",' said Melba.

So that is what went off:

REGRET INDISPOSED.   TOUCHED THOUGHT.

But alas what arrived was rather different:

REGRET INDISPOSED.   TOUCHED PORT.

Nichols adds that the money spent on the orchids was worth it: the hostess dined out on the story for weeks.

Helena Rubinstein was rich and meant to stay that way. When her husband, Prince Gourielli, died in 1955 she decided not to go to the funeral in New York. 'He's dead,' she said. 'Why waste the money?'

Instead she told Patrick O'Higgins, later to become her biographer, to send a telegram to her son. She dictated it:

YOUR MOTHER TOO SICK TO TRAVEL. PLEASE MAKE SUITABLE ARRANGEMENTS AND SEND FLOWERS ON HER BEHALF.

Mr O'Higgins was on his way when madame called him back. 'He's dead, there's no hurry,' she said. 'See that you send it night letter.'

That halved the cost.

VICTORIANA

The electric telegraph began life the year Queen Victoria came to the throne and in time they were to celebrate their diamond jubilees together.

Like her subjects, the Queen came to love and rely on telegrams and she sent them on occasions great and small. Indeed when Lord Hartington, Gladstone's War Minister, had the temerity to suggest that perhaps she should not have telegraphed direct to Lord Wolseley in the Sudan, she was furious.

'The Queen always *has* telegraphed direct to her Generals, and *always will* do so . . .' she wrote in reply, 'but she thinks Lord Hartington's letter *very officious* and *impertinent in tone.* The Queen *has* the *right* to telegraph congratulations and enquiries to *any* one . . .'

She certainly exercised that right and Lord Hartington could not have been the only Minister to have wished that the coming of the electric telegraph had been somewhat delayed. Here she is, for instance, in urgent touch with her Prime Minister on the subject of Jack the Ripper.

Queen Victoria to the Marquess of Salisbury, Balmoral Castle, 10 November 1888:

THIS NEW MOST GHASTLY MURDER SHOWS THE ABSOLUTE NECESSITY FOR SOME VERY DECIDED ACTION. ALL THESE COURTS MUST BE LIT AND OUR DETECTIVES IMPROVED. THEY ARE NOT WHAT THEY SHOULD BE. YOU PROMISED WHEN THE FIRST MURDER TOOK PLACE TO CONSULT WITH YOUR COLLEAGUES ABOUT IT.

The Marquess of Salisbury to Queen Victoria, 10 November 1888:

HUMBLE DUTY. AT CABINET TODAY IT WAS RESOLVED TO ISSUE A
PROCLAMATION OFFERING FREE PARDON TO ANYONE WHO SHOULD GIVE
EVIDENCE AS TO THE RECENT MURDER EXCEPT THE ACTUAL PERPETRATOR
OF THE CRIME.

And here she is, from her holiday hotel in the south of France, expressing herself
on a burning topic of the day:

    Queen Victoria to Lieutenant-Colonel Bigge, Grand Hotel de Cimiez, 23
March 1895:

THE QUEEN IS HORRIFIED AT THE MOTION FOR PAYMENT OF M.P.S BEING
CARRIED. WHERE IS THE MONEY TO COME FROM? IT WILL LOWER THE
HOUSE OF COMMONS, ALREADY SO MUCH SPOILT, STILL MORE, BUT SHE
CANNOT THINK IT WILL BE FINALLY AGREED TO OR CARRIED.

The holiday itself was not without its moments of alarm.

The Earl of Rosebery to Queen Victoria, 29 March 1895:

HUMBLE DUTY. I FEAR WE ARE RAPIDLY APPROACHING A CONDITION OF SEVERE TENSION WITH THE FRENCH GOVT OWING TO ITS STRANGE PROCEEDINGS IN AFRICA AND SIAM. A CABINET IS SUMMONED FOR TOMORROW WHICH MAY PROVE CRITICAL BUT I HOPE THE CRISIS MAY BE TIDED OVER.

Queen Victoria to the Earl of Rosebery, 29 March 1895:

YOUR TELEGRAM RATHER DISQUIETING. WHILE TRUSTING THAT THE GOVT WILL PRESERVE A STRONG ATTITUDE AGAINST FRENCH ENCROACHMENTS I HOPE CRISIS MAY BE AVERTED ON NATIONAL GROUNDS AND ALSO THAT PERSONALLY IT WOULD BE VERY AWKWARD IF COMPLICATIONS AROSE WITH A COUNTRY IN WHICH I AM NOW RESIDING AND RECEIVING MARKED COURTESY AND ATTENTION.

Queen Victoria was passionately concerned about the fate of General Gordon. Holed up in Khartoum, Gordon may have lacked many things but he had the electric telegraph. Here he is answering a query from the Foreign Secretary:

General Gordon to Lord Granville:

YOU ASK ME TO STATE CAUSE AND INTENTION IN STAYING AT KHARTOUM KNOWING GOVERNMENT MEANS TO ABANDON SUDAN AND IN ANSWER I SAY I STAY AT KHARTOUM BECAUSE THE ARABS HAVE SHUT US UP AND WILL NOT LET US OUT.

And when he was speared to death, Gladstone, Granville and Hartington all received an identical telegram from their Queen. No code was used so that all who saw it might read her bitter words:

THESE NEWS FROM KHARTOUM ARE FRIGHTFUL AND TO THINK THAT ALL THIS MIGHT HAVE BEEN PREVENTED AND MANY PRECIOUS LIVES SAVED BY EARLIER ACTION IS TOO FRIGHTFUL.

In 1887 the old Queen and the electric telegraph were celebrating their diamond jubilees. Her message to her worldwide empire went out:

FROM MY HEART I THANK MY BELOVED PEOPLE. MAY GOD BLESS THEM.

HANDCUFFS, LONDON

The dramatic arrest of Dr Crippen in Montreal on 31 July 1910 was a landmark in criminal detection. It was the first time the police had used the new invention of wireless telegraphy.

Scotland Yard had been alerted by this famous message from Captain Kendall, master of the *Montrose,* in mid-Atlantic:

Captain Kendall, *Montrose,* to Scotland Yard, 22 July 1910:

HAVE STRONG SUSPICIONS THAT CRIPPEN LONDON CELLAR MURDERER AND ACCOMPLICE ARE AMONGST SALOON PASSENGERS MOUSTACHE TAKEN OFF GROWING BEARD ACCOMPLICE DRESSED AS BOY VOICE MANNER AND BUILD UNDOUBTEDLY A GIRL BOTH TRAVELLING AS MR AND MASTER ROBINSON.

Chief Inspector Walter Dew caught a faster ship to Quebec and was waiting at Montreal when the *Montrose* arrived. Captain Kendall kept in close touch.

Captain Kendall to Chief Inspector Dew, 30 July 1910:

ADVISE YOU TO COME OFF IN SMALL BOAT WITH PILOT DISGUISED AS ONE IF POSSIBLE.

Chief Inspector Dew to Captain Kendall, 30 July 1910:

THANKS WILL SPEAK YOU LATER OPERATOR HERE WILL MAKE ARRANGEMENTS.
MEANTIME SUGGEST SUSPECTS KEPT UNDER DISCREET OBSERVATION TO
PREVENT SUICIDE.

Captain Kendall to Chief Inspector Dew, 31 July 1910:

TELL CAPTAIN OF PILOT STEAMER TO STEAM WITH REPORTERS TOWARDS
BIG ISLAND...UNTIL I HOIST A CANADIAN ENSIGN AT MAINMAST
INDICATING YOU HAVE MADE THE ARREST.

To Handcuffs, London, England, 31 July 1910:

CRIPPEN AND LENEVE ARRESTED WIRE LATER DEW.

Handcuffs, London, was and still is the telegraphic address of Scotland Yard.

Sixty-four years later the thirteen telegrams that led to Dr Crippen's arrest were auctioned in London. Scotland Yard wanted them for its Police Museum and sent an officer along with £100. Bidding started higher than that and the telegrams were eventually sold for £1,600.

CABLED HEADS OF EUROPE

Three notorious German telegrams have found a place in the history books. Each upset a delicately balanced apple cart.

The first was known as the Ems telegram because King William of Prussia, who sent it, was taking the waters at Ems at the time.

It reported a chance meeting between the King and the French Ambassador on the promenade. The Ambassador had made demands of the King: he said he must renounce the claims of the House of Hohenzollern to the throne of Spain forever. The King declined to do so, raised his hat and went in to lunch.

His telegram, offensively reworded and issued far and wide by Bismarck, sparked off the Franco-Prussian War. No one was more surprised than King William.

Then there was the Kaiser's telegram to Kruger after the Jameson Raid. This was how it read:

The Emperor Wilhelm II to President Kruger, 11.20 a.m. 3 January 1896:

I EXPRESS MY SINCERE CONGRATULATIONS THAT, SUPPORTED BY YOUR PEOPLE, WITHOUT APPEALING FOR THE HELP OF FRIENDLY POWERS, YOU HAVE SUCCEEDED BY YOUR OWN ENERGETIC ACTION AGAINST ARMED BANDS WHICH INVADED YOUR COUNTRY AS DISTURBERS OF THE PEACE, AND HAVE THUS BEEN ENABLED TO RESTORE PEACE AND SAFEGUARD THE INDEPENDENCE OF THE COUNTRY AGAINST ATTACKS FROM THE OUTSIDE. WILHELM IR

Few telegrams can ever have raised such a storm. Britain was swept by a blaze of anti-German feeling. The Queen was outraged, the Government mobilised the fleet and the Jameson Raid had, in an instant, become an international incident.

The third ill-judged telegram was the Zimmermann telegram. This one, most usefully for the Allies, helped to get the United States at last into the First World War.

Zimmermann was the German Foreign Secretary and here is his telegram:

FOREIGN MINISTER TO COUNT VON BERNSTORFF, AMBASSADOR TO WASHINGTON. WE INTEND TO BEGIN UNRESTRICTED SUBMARINE WARFARE ON THE FIRST OF FEBRUARY. WE SHALL ENDEAVOUR IN SPITE OF THIS TO KEEP UNITED STATES NEUTRAL. IN THE EVENT OF THIS NOT SUCCEEDING, WE MAKE MEXICO A PROPOSAL OF ALLIANCE ON THE FOLLOWING BASIS: MAKE WAR TOGETHER, MAKE PEACE TOGETHER, GENEROUS FINANCIAL SUPPORT, AND AN UNDERSTANDING ON OUR PART THAT MEXICO IS TO RECONQUER THE LOST TERRITORY IN TEXAS, NEW MEXICO, AND ARIZONA. THE SETTLEMENT IN DETAIL IS LEFT TO YOU.

YOU WILL INFORM THE PRESIDENT (of Mexico) OF THE ABOVE MOST SECRETLY AS SOON AS THE OUTBREAK OF WAR WITH THE UNITED STATES IS CERTAIN AND AT THE SUGGESTION THAT HE SHOULD, ON HIS OWN INITIATIVE, INVITE JAPAN TO IMMEDIATE ADHERENCE AND AT THE SAME TIME MEDIATE BETWEEN JAPAN AND OURSELVES.

PLEASE CALL THE PRESIDENT'S ATTENTION TO THE FACT THAT THE UNRESTRICTED EMPLOYMENT OF OUR SUBMARINES NOW OFFERS THE PROSPECT OF COMPELLING ENGLAND TO MAKE PEACE WITHIN A FEW MONTHS. ACKNOWLEDGE RECEIPT. ZIMMERMANN

The telegram was intercepted by British Naval Intelligence and decoded at once. The British had broken the German code early in the war and the Germans never thought to change it, thus saving everyone a lot of trouble. It was passed to the American Ambassador to London, who sent it straight to President Wilson, who stopped talking about mediating and released it to the press.

America was outraged and on 6 April declared war.

In the long hot summer of 1914, as Europe hurtled towards war, telegrams from two interested parties crossed...

Wilhelm II, Kaiser of Germany, to Nicholas II, Tsar of Russia, July 1914:

IT IS WITH THE GREATEST CONCERN THAT I HEAR OF THE IMPRESSION WHICH THE ACTION OF AUSTRIA AGAINST SERBIA IS CREATING IN YOUR COUNTRY. THE UNSCRUPULOUS AGITATION THAT HAS BEEN GOING ON IN SERBIA FOR YEARS HAS RESULTED IN THE OUTRAGEOUS CRIME TO WHICH ARCHDUKE FRANZ FERDINAND FELL VICTIM... WILLY

Nicholas II, Tsar of Russia, to Wilhelm II, Kaiser of Germany, July 1914:

AM GLAD YOU ARE BACK. IN THIS MOST SERIOUS MOMENT I APPEAL TO YOU TO HELP ME. AN IGNOBLE WAR HAS BEEN DECLARED ON A WEAK COUNTRY. THE INDIGNATION IN RUSSIA, SHARED FULLY BY ME, IS ENORMOUS. I FORESEE THAT VERY SHORTLY SOON I SHALL BE OVERWHELMED BY PRESSURE BROUGHT UPON ME AND FORCED TO TAKE EXTREME MEASURES WHICH WILL LEAD TO WAR. TO TRY AND AVOID SUCH A CALAMITY AS A EUROPEAN WAR I BEG YOU IN THE NAME OF OUR OLD FRIENDSHIP TO DO WHAT YOU CAN TO STOP YOUR ALLIES FROM GOING TOO FAR. NICKY

Wilhelm II, Kaiser of Germany, to Nicholas II, Tsar of Russia, 29 July 1914:

IT WOULD BE QUITE POSSIBLE FOR RUSSIA TO REMAIN A SPECTATOR OF
THE AUSTRO-SERBIAN CONFLICT WITHOUT INVOLVING EUROPE IN THE MOST
HORRIBLE WAR SHE EVER WITNESSED...OF COURSE MILITARY MEASURES ON
THE PART OF RUSSIA WHICH WOULD BE LOOKED UPON BY AUSTRIA AS
THREATENING WOULD PRECIPITATE A CALAMITY WE BOTH WISH TO AVOID...
WILLY

Nicholas II, Tsar of Russia, to Wilhelm II, Kaiser of Germany, 29 July 1914:

I THANK YOU FOR YOUR CONCILIATORY AND FRIENDLY TELEGRAM WHEREAS
THE COMMUNICATIONS OF YOUR AMBASSADOR TO MY MINISTER TODAY
HAVE BEEN IN A VERY DIFFERENT TONE. PLEASE CLEAR UP THIS
DIFFERENCE... NICHOLAS

Wilhelm II, Kaiser of Germany, to Nicholas II, Tsar of Russia, 30 July 1914:

I HAVE GONE TO THE UTMOST LIMITS OF THE POSSIBLE IN MY EFFORTS
TO SAVE PEACE. IT IS NOT I WHO WILL BEAR THE RESPONSIBILITY FOR
THE TERRIBLE DISASTER WHICH NOW THREATENS THE CIVILISED WORLD.
YOU AND YOU ALONE CAN STILL AVERT IT. MY FRIENDSHIP FOR YOU AND
YOUR EMPIRE WHICH MY GRANDFATHER BEQUEATHED TO ME ON HIS

DEATHBED IS STILL SACRED TO ME AND I HAVE BEEN LOYAL TO RUSSIA
WHEN SHE WAS IN TROUBLE, NOTABLY DURING YOUR LAST WAR. EVEN
NOW YOU CAN SAVE THE PEACE OF EUROPE BY STOPPING YOUR MILITARY
MEASURES. WILLY

Nicholas II, Tsar of Russia, to Wilhelm II, Kaiser of Germany, 1 August 1914:

I UNDERSTAND THAT YOU ARE COMPELLED TO MOBILISE BUT I SHOULD
LIKE TO HAVE THE SAME GUARANTEE FROM YOU THAT I GAVE YOU MYSELF
— THAT THESE MEASURES DO NOT MEAN WAR AND THAT WE SHALL CONTINUE
TO NEGOTIATE TO SAVE THE GENERAL PEACE SO DEAR TO OUR HEARTS...
NICKY

That evening Germany declared war on Russia.

The war began well for Russia. The Tsar enjoyed himself visiting troops and hospitals and handing out icons. There were even some victories.

Tsar Nicholas to Tsaritsa Alexandra, 23 October 1914:

THE JOYFUL NEWS HAS BEEN RECEIVED THAT THE AUSTRIAN ARMY IS IN FULL RETREAT FROM SANOK. AM GOING TO A MOLEBEN (Te Deum) NOW. EMBRACE YOU CLOSELY. NICKY

Tsar Nicholas to Tsaritsa Alexandra, 9 March 1915:

PRZEMYSL IS TAKEN. PRAISE BE TO GOD! NICKY

But victories were few. Indeed, by the summer of 1915 the Russians were in full retreat with losses of nearly four million. There had never been a slaughter like it in the history of war. There was never a hint of this, though, in the Tsar's telegrams home.

Tsar Nicholas to Tsaritsa Alexandra, 14 October 1915:

YESTERDAY SPENT AN UNFORGETTABLE DAY AMONG THE TROOPS. THE IMPRESSIONS ARE OF THE VERY BEST... NICKY

Tsar Nicholas to Tsaritsa Alexandra, 29 October 1915:

INSPECTED THREE REGIMENTS OF VARIOUS SIBERIAN TROOPS AND THE
CAVALRY BEHIND RIGA. IT IS WARM, RAINY, NO SNOW. WENT TO A
LARGE, BEAUTIFUL HOSPITAL. HEARD FIRING IN THE DISTANCE. THE
IMPRESSIONS ARE VERY GOOD... NICKY

Tsar Nicholas to Tsaritsa Alexandra, 19 December 1915:

WARMEST THANKS FOR DEAR LETTER. I AM GLAD THE LITTLE ONE IS ON
HIS FEET AGAIN. FANCY, GEORGIE HAS PROMOTED ME TO FIELD-MARSHAL
OF THE BRITISH ARMY... NICKY

The Tsaritsa wrote endlessly. Every day the letters arrived, advising, cajoling, urging him to get rid of this minister and that general, always imploring him to listen to 'Our Friend': Rasputin. She cabled 'Their Friend', too.

Tsaritsa Alexandra to Rasputin (undated):

```
I CANNOT BEAR YOUR ABSENCE.  LIFE IS SO GREY AND HOPELESS
WITHOUT YOU MY DEAR COMFORTER, MY MASTER.  ALEXIS HAS BEEN TAKEN
ILL.  DO NOT TAKE ANY NOTICE OF KOKOVTSOV.  HE IS RESPONSIBLE
FOR MY HASTY WORDS TO YOU AND SHALL SUFFER FOR IT. FORGIVE ME.
RETURN FOR MY SAKE AND FOR THE LIFE OF ALEXIS.  A
```

And the Tsar himself had pleaded with him by telegram:

```
FRIEND, I CANNOT COMMAND BUT I BEG OF YOU TO RETURN INSTANTLY TO
US.  WE WANT YOUR HELP.  WITHOUT IT ALEXIS WILL DIE AND THE
HOUSE OF ROMANOFF IS DOOMED.  I HAVE SENT THE IMPERIAL TRAIN FOR
YOU.  IT LEAVES IN AN HOUR.  NICHOLAS
```

Now something dreadful happened to 'Our Friend' and the Empress was beside herself:

```
I AM WORRIED BY THE AWFUL RUMOURS.  NO DETAILS.  REMEMBER WHAT
I WROTE TO YOU.  ALIX
```

And:

NO TRACE YET. THE POLICE ARE CONTINUING THE SEARCH. I FEAR
THAT THESE TWO WRETCHED BOYS HAVE COMMITTED A FRIGHTFUL CRIME
BUT HAVE NOT YET LOST ALL HOPE. START TODAY. I NEED YOU
TERRIBLY.

And:

FATHER IS NO MORE. PUNISH THE ENEMIES OF RUSSIA AND OF OUR
HOUSE. COME BACK AT ONCE. I CAN BEAR IT NO LONGER. ALIX

On 30 December 1916 the Tsar replied:

AM HORRIFIED AND SHAKEN. IN PRAYER AND THOUGHTS I AM WITH YOU.
AM ARRIVING TOMORROW AT 5 O'CLOCK. HEAVY FROST. THE CONFERENCE
CLOSED AT 4 O'CLOCK. I BLESS YOU AND KISS YOU. NICKY

It was in the New Year of 1917 that Rasputin's body was found in the river.

The Tsar returned to Petrograd. Crisis piled high upon crisis and early in March he set out for the front again. Five days later the imperial government collapsed. But the Tsar's telegrams had resumed their extraordinary tone of mild domesticity:

Tsar Nicholas to Tsaritsa Alexandra, 10 March 1917:

WHAT A NUISANCE! I WAS HOPING THEY WOULD ESCAPE MEASLES. SINCEREST GREETINGS TO ALL. SLEEP WELL. NICKY

The next day the Tsar got a telegram from the President of the Duma:

THE POSITION IS SERIOUS. THERE IS ANARCHY IN THE CAPITAL. THE GOVERNMENT IS PARALYSED. TRANSPORTATION OF FOOD AND FUEL IS COMPLETELY DISORGANISED... THERE IS DISORDERLY FIRING IN THE STREETS. A PERSON TRUSTED BY THE COUNTRY MUST BE CHARGED IMMEDIATELY TO FORM A MINISTRY. MAY THE BLAME NOT FALL ON THE WEARER OF THE CROWN. RODZIANKO

And the day after that:

Tsaritsa Alexandra to Tsar Nicholas, 12 March 1917:

CONCESSIONS INEVITABLE. STREET FIGHTING CONTINUES. MANY UNITS GONE OVER TO THE ENEMY. ALIX

And the day after *that:*

Rodzianko to General Ruzsky, 13 March 1917:

HIS MAJESTY AND YOURSELF APPARENTLY ARE UNABLE TO REALISE WHAT IS HAPPENING IN THE CAPITAL. A TERRIBLE REVOLUTION HAS BROKEN OUT. HATRED OF THE EMPRESS HAS REACHED A FEVER PITCH. TO PREVENT BLOODSHED I HAVE BEEN FORCED TO ARREST ALL THE MINISTERS. DON'T SEND ANY MORE TROOPS. I AM HANGING FROM A THREAD MYSELF. POWER IS SLIPPING FROM MY HANDS. THE MEASURES YOU PROPOSE ARE TOO LATE. THE TIME FOR THEM IS GONE. THERE IS NO RETURN.

The following day the Imperial train was diverted to Pskow and the Tsar sent his wife the last telegram of his reign. Not a hint of his troubles are in it.

Tsar Nicholas to Tsaritsa Alexandra, 14 March 1917:

ARRIVED HERE AT DINNER-TIME. HOPE THAT EVERYBODY'S HEALTH IS BETTER AND THAT WE SHALL SOON SEE EACH OTHER. CLOSE EMBRACE. NICKY

The Tsar abdicated the next day. In another week he was arrested. Ahead lay a long and increasingly difficult imprisonment and at last, for him and all his family, death in the cellar at Ekaterinburg.

Meanwhile, from Great Britain where the Tsar's cousin, George V, reigned, came the reaction of the British Government:

David Lloyd George, Prime Minister of Great Britain to Prince Lvov, Prime Minister of the Provisional Government of Russia:

IT IS WITH SENTIMENTS OF THE PROFOUNDEST SATISFACTION THAT THE PEOPLE OF GREAT BRITAIN...HAVE LEARNED THAT THEIR GREAT ALLY RUSSIA NOW STANDS WITH THE NATIONS WHICH BASE THEIR INSTITUTIONS UPON RESPONSIBLE GOVERNMENT... WE BELIEVE THAT THE REVOLUTION IS THE GREATEST SERVICE WHICH THEY HAVE YET MADE TO THE CAUSE FOR WHICH THE ALLIED PEOPLES HAVE BEEN FIGHTING SINCE AUGUST 1914. IT REVEALS THE FUNDAMENTAL TRUTH THAT THIS WAR IS AT BOTTOM A STRUGGLE FOR POPULAR GOVERNMENT AS WELL AS FOR LIBERTY.

Hitler spent his last days in the bunker in Berlin and while Russian troops encircled the ruined city, cutting it off completely, telegrams still came in and went out...

An ill-judged telegram arrived from Goering:

```
MY FUEHRER!
IN VIEW OF YOUR DECISION TO REMAIN IN THE FORTRESS OF BERLIN, DO
YOU AGREE THAT I TAKE OVER AT ONCE THE TOTAL LEADERSHIP OF THE
REICH, WITH FULL FREEDOM OF ACTION AT HOME AND ABROAD AS YOUR
DEPUTY, IN ACCORDANCE WITH YOUR DECREE OF JUNE 29, 1941?  IF NO
REPLY IS RECEIVED BY TEN O'CLOCK TONIGHT, I SHALL TAKE IT FOR
GRANTED THAT YOU HAVE LOST YOUR FREEDOM OF ACTION, AND SHALL
CONSIDER THE CONDITIONS OF YOUR DECREE AS FULFILLED, AND SHALL
ACT FOR THE BEST INTERESTS OF OUR COUNTRY AND OUR PEOPLE.  YOU
KNOW WHAT I FEEL FOR YOU IN THIS GRAVEST HOUR OF MY LIFE.  WORDS
FAIL ME TO EXPRESS MYSELF.  MAY GOD PROTECT YOU, AND SPEED YOU
QUICKLY HERE IN SPITE OF ALL.
                          YOUR LOYAL
                          HERMANN GOERING
```

Hitler was enraged and dictated telegrams accusing the Reichsmarschall of high treason, stripping him of all his offices, ordering his arrest.

Hitler's orders, as always, were obeyed. Goering and his advisers were arrested the next day.

By the end of the week the Russians were fighting in the streets of Berlin and the telegrams from the bunker grew ever more frantic.

Hitler to General Feldmarschall Keitel, 28 April 1945:

```
I EXPECT THE RELIEF OF BERLIN.  WHAT IS HEINRICI'S ARMY DOING?
WHERE IS WENCK?  WHAT IS HAPPENING TO THE NINTH ARMY?  WHEN
WILL WENCK AND THE NINTH ARMY JOIN?
```

Martin Bormann to Grand Admiral Doenitz, 30 April 1945:

```
DOENITZ!  OUR IMPRESSION GROWS DAILY STRONGER THAT THE DIVISIONS
IN THE BERLIN THEATRE HAVE BEEN STANDING IDLE FOR SEVERAL DAYS.
ALL THE REPORTS WE RECEIVE ARE CONTROLLED, SUPPRESSED OR
DISTORTED BY KEITEL.  IN GENERAL WE CAN ONLY COMMUNICATE THROUGH
KEITEL.  THE FUEHRER ORDERS YOU TO PROCEED AT ONCE, AND
MERCILESSLY, AGAINST ALL TRAITORS.  BORMANN.  THE FUEHRER IS
ALIVE AND IS CONDUCTING THE DEFENCE OF BERLIN.
```

That afternoon Hitler shot himself, Eva Braun took poison and their bodies were carried from the bunker, soaked in petrol and burned.

There was no mention of this in the telegram Martin Bormann now sent.
Martin Bormann to Grand Admiral Doenitz:

IN PLACE OF THE FORMER REICHSMARSCHALL GOERING THE FUEHRER
APPOINTS YOU, HERR GRAND ADMIRAL, AS HIS SUCCESSOR. WRITTEN
AUTHORITY IS ON ITS WAY. YOU WILL IMMEDIATELY TAKE ALL SUCH
MEASURES AS THE SITUATION REQUIRES. BORMANN

Doenitz was dismayed. He didn't want the job. So was Himmler. He did. But both
thought Hitler was still alive and both leapt to do his bidding.
Grand Admiral Doenitz to Hitler:

MY FUEHRER! MY LOYALTY TO YOU WILL BE UNCONDITIONAL. I SHALL
DO EVERYTHING POSSIBLE TO RELIEVE YOU IN BERLIN. IF FATE
NEVERTHELESS COMPELS ME TO RULE THE REICH AS YOUR APPOINTED
SUCCESSOR I SHALL CONTINUE THIS WAR TO AN END WORTHY OF THE
UNIQUE HEROIC STRUGGLE OF THE GERMAN PEOPLE.

The following day there were two more telegrams for the Admiral.
Martin Bormann to Grand Admiral Doenitz, 1 May 1945:

THE TESTAMENT IS IN FORCE. I WILL JOIN YOU AS SOON AS POSSIBLE.
TILL THEN I RECOMMEND THAT PUBLICATION BE HELD UP. BORMANN

And that afternoon:

Dr Joseph Goebbels to Grand Admiral Doenitz:

MOST SECRET - URGENT - OFFICER ONLY. THE FUEHRER DIED YESTERDAY AT 15.30 HOURS. TESTAMENT OF 29 APRIL APPOINTS YOU AS REICH PRESIDENT, REICH MINISTER DR GOEBBELS AS REICH CHANCELLOR, REICHSLEITER BORMANN AS PARTY MINISTER, REICH MINISTER SEYSS-INQUART AS FOREIGN MINISTER. BY ORDER OF THE FUEHRER THE TESTAMENT HAS BEEN SENT OUT OF BERLIN TO YOU, TO FIELD MARSHAL SCHOERNER AND FOR PRESERVATION AND PUBLICATION. REICHSLEITER BORMANN INTENDS TO GO TO YOU TODAY AND TO INFORM YOU OF THE SITUATION. TIME AND FORM OF ANNOUNCEMENT TO THE PRESS AND TO THE TROOPS IS LEFT TO YOU. CONFIRM RECEIPT. GOEBBELS

Dr Goebbels and his wife shot their six children and then themselves.

Martin Bormann slipped away through the ruins.

CHURCHILL KEEPS IT SHORT

When the American telegraph was in its infancy, President Polk was asked to test it, which he did with the world's longest telegram: 50,000 words. It took twenty-four hours to transmit.

Brevity, President Polk, that is what the telegraph is all about, as Winston Churchill so often said. Mind you, Churchill's own telegrams went on a bit. But Saviours of the Nation are allowed an extra word or two.

Churchill to British Secretary of State for Foreign Affairs, 11 January 1941:

YOU SPOKE TO ME THE OTHER DAY ABOUT THE LENGTH OF TELEGRAMS. I FEEL THAT THIS IS AN EVIL WHICH OUGHT TO BE CHECKED. MINISTERS AND AMBASSADORS ABROAD SEEM TO THINK THAT THE BIGGER THE VOLUME OF THEIR REPORTS HOME THE BETTER IS THEIR TASK DISCHARGED. ALL KINDS OF GOSSIP AND RUMOURS ARE SENT, REGARDLESS OF CREDIBILITY. THE IDEA SEEMS TO BE TO KEEP UP A CONTINUED CHAT WHICH NO ONE EVER TRIES TO SHORTEN. I SUGGEST THAT YOU SHOULD ISSUE A GENERAL INJUNCTION BUT THAT IN ADDITION TELEGRAMS WHICH ARE UNDULY VERBOSE OR TRIVIAL SHOULD BE CRITICISED AS SUCH AND THEIR AUTHORS TOLD 'THIS TELEGRAM WAS NEEDLESSLY LONG'. IT IS SHEER LAZINESS NOT COMPRESSING THOUGHT INTO A REASONABLE SPACE. I TRY TO READ ALL THESE TELEGRAMS AND I THINK THE VOLUME GROWS FROM DAY TO DAY. PLEASE LET ME KNOW WHAT CAN BE DONE.

Winston Churchill to British Secretary of State for India, 15 October 1941:

KINDLY LET ME KNOW HOW MANY WORDS HIS MAJESTY'S REPRESENTATIVE
AT KABUL HAS TELEGRAPHED SINCE THE DAY WHEN THE QUESTION OF
TURNING THE GERMANS OUT OF AFGHANISTAN WAS FIRST MENTIONED TO
HIM.

Winston Churchill to His Majesty's representative at Kabul, 19 October 1941:

I HAVE BEEN MUCH PLEASED WITH THE WAY IN WHICH YOU HAVE HANDLED
THE QUESTION OF TURNING OUT THE GERMANS AND ITALIANS, BUT I
THINK YOU OUGHT TO KNOW THAT FROM SEPTEMBER 11, WHEN THIS TASK
WAS ENTRUSTED TO YOU, TO OCTOBER 17, YOU HAVE SENT 6,639 CIPHER
GROUPS. THE LABOUR AND COST OF THIS PROFUSE TELEGRAPHING AND
THE CHOKING EFFECT OF SUCH LENGTHY MESSAGES UPON THE HIGHER
ADMINISTRATION OUGHT NEVER TO BE FORGOTTEN. CLARITY AND COGENCY
CAN, I AM SURE, BE RECONCILED WITH A GREATER BREVITY.

Churchill to Minister of Information, 29 August 1941:

DO TRY TO BLEND IN WITHOUT CAUSING TROUBLE THE WORD PERSIA
INSTEAD OF IRAN.

Churchill to Foreign Secretary, 18 January 1941:

IF YOU APPROVE I SHOULD LIKE LIVORNO TO BE CALLED IN THE ENGLISH
– LEGHORN: AND ISTANBUL IN ENGLISH – CONSTANTINOPLE. OF COURSE,
WHEN SPEAKING OR WRITING TURKISH WE CAN USE THE TURKISH NAME;
AND IF AT ANY TIME YOU ARE CONVERSING AGREEABLY WITH MUSSOLINI
IN ITALIAN LIVORNO WOULD BE CORRECT. AND WHY IS SIAM BURIED
UNDER THE NAME OF THAILAND?

Prime Minister to the First Lord, 27 January 1942:

IS IT REALLY NECESSARY TO DESCRIBE THE TIRPITZ AS THE ADMIRAL
VON TIRPITZ IN EVERY SIGNAL? THIS MUST CAUSE A CONSIDERABLE
WASTE OF TIME FOR SIGNALMEN, CIPHER STAFF AND TYPISTS. SURELY
TIRPITZ IS GOOD ENOUGH FOR THE BEAST?

And here is perhaps the most celebrated exchange of telegrams of the war:

Winston Churchill to General Alexander, Commander-in-Chief, Middle East, 10 August 1942:

YOUR PRIME AND MAIN DUTY WILL BE TO TAKE OR DESTROY AT THE EARLIEST OPPORTUNITY THE GERMAN-ITALIAN ARMY COMMANDED BY FIELD-MARSHAL ROMMEL, TOGETHER WITH ALL ITS SUPPLIES AND ESTABLISHMENTS IN EGYPT AND LIBYA.
2. YOU WILL DISCHARGE OR CAUSE TO BE DISCHARGED SUCH OTHER DUTIES AS PERTAIN TO YOUR COMMAND WITHOUT PREJUDICE TO THE TASK DESCRIBED IN PARAGRAPH 1 WHICH MUST BE CONSIDERED PARAMOUNT IN HIS MAJESTY'S INTERESTS.

General Alexander to Churchill, undated but sent on 4 February 1943:

SIR, THE ORDERS YOU GAVE ME ON AUGUST 10 1942 HAVE BEEN FULFILLED. HIS MAJESTY'S ENEMIES, TOGETHER WITH THEIR IMPEDIMENTA, HAVE BEEN COMPLETELY ELIMINATED FROM EGYPT CYRENAICA, LIBYA AND TRIPOLITANIA. I NOW AWAIT YOUR FURTHER INSTRUCTIONS.

A FEW GOOD BITS FROM THE BIBLE

Senior British fighting men do well to pack their bibles. Otherwise they don't understand half the cables. For instance...

Churchill to General Wavell after his victories in Libya, 18 December 1940:
ST MATTHEW, CHAPTER VII, VERSE 7.
('Ask and it shall be given you; seek and ye shall find; knock and it shall be opened unto you.')

General Wavell to Churchill, 19 December 1940:
ST JAMES, CHAPTER 1, FIRST PART OF VERSE 17.
('Every good gift and every perfect gift is from above...')

Allies do well to keep a bible handy too.

In November 1943 President Roosevelt, preparing for a summit conference, telegraphed Churchill to say that his security advisers thought Cairo too dangerous. He received this telegram.

Prime Minister to President:

SEE ST JOHN, CHAPTER XIV, VERSES 1 TO 4.

('Let not your heart be troubled; ye believe in God, believe also in me. In my Father's house are many mansions; if it were not so I would have told you. I go to prepare a place for you. And if I go and prepare a place for you I will come again and receive you unto myself; that where I am there ye may be also. And whither I go ye know and the way ye know.')

The conference was held in Cairo.

Sir Robert Menzies in choppy seas aboard the Norwegian freighter *Halibut* with his equally seasick wife and daughter:

EXODUS X, 23.

('They saw not one another, neither rose any from his place for three days.')

Soprano Frances Alda had been queen of the Metropolitan for more than twenty years and after her retirement from the stage she often sang on the radio. Her programme, however, hardly ever varied and one day a cable came from her agent:

HEBREWS XIII. 8.

She looked up the reference in her Bible and found these words: 'Jesus Christ, the same yesterday, and to day, and for ever.'

FURTHER TO MY LAST SIX WIRES...

The Russians hold the world telegram-sending record. In 1975 they sent 443,482,000 telegrams, narrowly beating the previous record held by Mr Florenz Ziegfeld, the American impresario.

Mr Ziegfeld's flow of telegrams was prodigious: Western Union should have given him a medal. He would rather send a telegram than talk to you and sent thousands backstage to people he could have summoned in a minute. Like:

`ANY GIRL WHO CHANGES OR TWISTS HER HAT WILL BE FIRED.`

His telegrams were kept, passed round, wondered at. They could have come from no one else.

Here is a typical Ziegfeld telegram. It went to a publicity man called Bernard Sobel who had committed the ultimate crime of leaving to work for someone else. Ziegfeld thought this might lure him back:

I FORGIVE YOU FOR LEAVING ME PERHAPS NEXT TIME YOUR WORD WILL BE GOOD I WILL TRY TO DO ALL MY OWN PRESS WORK HEREAFTER AS I HAVE NOTHING TO DO AND CAN SAVE THREE SEVENTY FIVE WEEKLY PLUS FIFTY DOLLARS FOR EACH SHOW IN ALL FOUR TWENTY FIVE WEEKLY THAT IS WHAT I HAVE ASKED KINGSTON TO PAY YOU I HOPE YOUR POOR NERVES WILL SOON GET RESTED AFTER YOU LEAVE ME I SUPPOSE YOU ARE ALREADY EATING NOTHING BUT MATZOTH PLEASE SEND ME SIX BOXES ON THE 6.40 TRAIN TONIGHT WHEN DO YOU MOVE TO YOUR ABIES IRISH ROSE QUARTERS IN THE BRONX GOOD LUCK MY POOR MISGUIDED BEST PRESS AGENT IN THE WORLD. ZIEGFELD

And here is a telegram sent to Ring Lardner who had got involved with a show called *Smiles.*

The show was due to open in Boston and Lardner, in New York, was writing and rewriting lyrics up to the last minute, often to tunes whistled to him on the telephone by Vincent Youmans, the composer.

The Marilyn mentioned is Marilyn Miller, the star, and Lannin was Paul Lannin, the musical director:

LANNIN SAYS YOU LEFT OUT THE ENTIRE LINE IN THE RALLY ROUND ME
LYRIC MARILYN OBJECTS TO THE LINE ABOUT THE DEVIL AND LINE I
USED TO SHIRK MY WORK ETC I KNOW IT IS HARD TO WRITE A LYRIC
LONG DISTANCE AND IT IS HARD ON ME SO NEAR OPENING THIS IS A
TOUGH BUNCH TO HANDLE WILL YOU PHONE YOUMANS TO GET THE MUSIC
RIGHT I WAS FINALLY COMPELLED TO GET A COURT ORDER TO PREVENT
YOUMANS RUNNING THE SHOW THE ONLY THING HE FORGOT TO GIVE ME
A CHEQUE FOR 200,000 DOLLARS WE ARE GRADUALLY GETTING INTO SHAPE
AND WAYBURN IS DOING GREAT WORK AND THE COURT ORDER KEEPS
YOUMANS FROM INTERFERING THAT IS A VERY IMPORTANT LYRIC PLEASE
TRY AGAIN I THINK YOU HAVE GOT TOO MANY RALLY ROUND ME IN IT
REGARDS. ZIEGFELD

Ziegfeld's wife was the great Broadway and Hollywood star Billie Burke. If they were apart she got daily cables. Like:

MY DARLING YOURE NO DIFFERENT THAN ANY ONE ELSE ONLY YOU DONT KEEP STUBS TO YOUR CHECK BOOK. WHEN I LAY HERE ILL AS IVE BEEN YOU CHANGE YOUR MIND AND COME TO CONCLUSIONS NO MATTER HOW BAD THINGS ARE ITS GREAT TO BE ALIVE AND I DONT KNOW HOW IM GOING TO GET THROUGH. THINGS IN AMERICA ARE GETTING WORSE AND WORSE BUT DONT WORRY ALL MY LOVE.

Ziegfeld went on sending telegrams right to the end. His wife recalled in her autobiography that even as an invalid in Santa Monica, Ziegfeld ran up a telegram bill of $6,000 in the month before he died.

David O. Selznick, the Hollywood producer, was another wonderful customer of Western Union. He would never send a letter if he could send a cable.

Here he is giving his first reaction to a promising young actor.

David O. Selznick to B.P. Schulberg, General Manager of Paramount's West Coast production, 25 February 1931:

PLEASE WIRE INSTRUCTIONS CONCERNING LAURENCE OLIVIER AND JILL ESMOND. OPINION HERE DIVIDED WITH MAJORITY BELIEVING ESMOND MORE DESIRABLE FOR STOCK THAN OLIVIER. HOWEVER FELIX YOUNG AND

MYSELF ARE ONLY TWO THAT HAVE SEEN OLIVIER APART FROM TEST AND
WE BOTH CONSIDER HIM EXCELLENT POSSIBILITY. MY OWN FEELING IS
THAT, IN SPITE OF THEIR UNQUESTIONED MERIT, THEIR SALARY IS WAY
OUT OF LINE FOR BEGINNERS...

And here is his reaction to a promising young actress:

David O. Selznick to Katharine Brown (Story Editor in the New York office), 16
August 1938:

IN CONNECTION WITH BERGMAN WOULD STILL BE INTERESTED EVEN IF SHE
DOES NOT START UNTIL NEXT YEAR... IN CONNECTION WITH TERMS FOR
HER I MIGHT POINT OUT THAT SHE WAS NOT EVEN STARRED IN SWEDEN
SINCE THE MAIN TITLE OF 'INTERMEZZO' STARS GOSTA STEVENS AND
GUSTAF MOLANDER.
A COLD SHUDDER HAS JUST RUN THROUGH ME ON THE REALISATION THAT
MAYBE WE ARE DEALING FOR THE WRONG GIRL. MAYBE THE GIRL WE ARE
AFTER IS GOSTA STEVENS. YOU HAD BETTER CHECK ON THIS.

To Katharine Brown, 18 March 1939:

I NOTE BERGMAN IS 69½ INCHES TALL. IS IT POSSIBLE SHE IS
ACTUALLY THIS HIGH AND DO YOU THINK WE WILL HAVE TO USE
STEPLADDERS WITH LESLIE HOWARD?

David O. Selznick to director Richard Boleslawski during the filming of *The Garden of Allah*:

I AM GETTING TO THE END OF THE ROPE OF PATIENCE WITH CRITICISM BASED ON ASSUMPTION THAT ACTORS KNOW MORE ABOUT SCRIPTS THAN I DO, AND AM VERY DISTURBED, WORRIED AND UPSET BY TELEPHONE CALLS THAT ARE NOW POURING IN ON THE SCENE THAT PRECEDES THE CONFESSION WHICH DEFINITELY INDICATE THAT ANOTHER SITUATION IS BREWING OF THE SAME KIND THAT HAPPENED BEFORE WHERE THE ACTORS ARE GETTING TOGETHER AND GANGING UP ABOUT SCENES. WOULD APPRECIATE YOUR HAVING A FRANK HEART-TO-HEART TALK WITH MARLENE AND WITH BOYER... MARLENE'S PICTURES HAVE BEEN NOTORIOUS FOR THEIR GHASTLY WRITING. CHARLES IS YET TO HAVE AN OUTSTANDING AMERICAN PICTURE AND NEITHER OF THEM HAS EVER HAD A SINGLE PICTURE COMPARABLE WITH ANY ONE OF FIFTEEN THAT I HAVE MADE IN THE LAST YEARS. TELL THEM VERY BRUTALLY THAT THIS COMES FROM ME... IN THE STUDIO I WOULD HAVE A SHOWDOWN ON IT RIGHT NOW BUT SINCE IT IS ON LOCATION I MUST ASK AND EXPECT YOU TO DO IT NOT MERELY FOR ME BUT ALSO FOR YOURSELF. MAKE CLEAR TO THE ACTORS THAT IF THEY CHOOSE TO SULK THROUGH SCENES AND GIVE BAD PERFORMANCES I AM PERFECTLY PREPARED FOR THIS TOO AND AM NOT GOING TO ADD HUNDREDS OR THOUSANDS MORE TO A FABULOUS COST TO SATISFY THEIR TEMPERAMENT BUT WILL RELEASE THE PICTURE WITH

THOSE PERFORMANCES. I FEEL REINFORCED IN HAVING YOU WITH ME ON
THIS AND CAN THEREFORE TALK WITH CONVICTION AGAINST RIDICULOUS
ASSUMPTION THAT THEY KNOW ANYTHING ABOUT SCRIPT. IF THEY WILL
ONLY DO THEIR JOB AND GIVE A PERFORMANCE THAT WILL BE ENOUGH.
THAT IS ALL THAT THEY ARE BEING OVERPAID FOR.   DAVID

David O. Selznick to Katharine Brown, 25 May 1936:

HAVE GONE OVER AND CAREFULLY THOUGHT ABOUT GONE WITH THE WIND.
THINK IT IS FINE STORY AND I UNDERSTAND YOUR FEELING ABOUT IT.
IF WE HAD UNDER CONTRACT A WOMAN IDEALLY SUITED TO THE·LEAD I
WOULD PROBABLY BE MORE INCLINED TO BUY IT THAN I AM TODAY... I
FEEL, INCIDENTALLY, THAT ITS BACKGROUND IS VERY STRONGLY AGAINST
IT...

To Katharine Brown, 26 May 1936:

WANT YOU TO NOTE THAT I HAVE THOUGHT FURTHER ABOUT GONE WITH THE
WIND AND THE MORE I THINK ABOUT IT THE MORE I FEEL THERE IS AN
EXCELLENT PICTURE IN IT...

David O. Selznick to Mr Lowell V. Calvert, 15 June 1939:

WE ARE ABOUT TO CLOSE FOR LAURENCE OLIVIER FOR REBECCA BUT
BEFORE DOING SO ANXIOUS TO HAVE IMMEDIATE CHECK ON THE FOLLOWING:
...WILLIAM POWELL IS STILL EXTREMELY ANXIOUS TO PLAY THE PART:
HE WOULD COST $100,000 MORE THAN OLIVIER WHICH MEANS WE WOULD
HAVE TO GROSS $150,000 ADDITIONAL TO BREAK EVEN ON THE
EXPENDITURE... SINCE COLMAN IS THE ONLY PERFECT MAN AND WE
CANNOT GET HIM...THE DECISION SHOULD BE BASED SOLELY ON WHETHER
WILLIAM POWELL IS LIKELY TO ADD HUNDREDS OF THOUSANDS OF DOLLARS
TO THE GROSS...

Gertrude Lawrence was another great sender of telegrams. She carried telegram blanks around with her and sent telegrams to everyone she knew on all occasions.

Noël Coward once complained that her cables were arriving at all times of the day and night. When she first read *Private Lives* she dashed off a cable at once.

YOUR PLAY IS DELIGHTFUL AND THERE'S NOTHING THAT CAN'T BE FIXED.

Coward was not pleased. His reply read:

THE ONLY THING TO BE FIXED WILL BE YOUR PERFORMANCE.

Thirty more cables from Miss Lawrence followed.

Gertrude Lawrence to Lee Shubert (owner of a famous chain of theatres):

DEAR MR LEE: COULD YOU PLEASE DO SOMETHING ABOUT THE ELECTRIC SIGN AT THE ST JAMES THEATRE? I HAVE BEEN LADY IN THE DARK FOR THE KING AND I FOR OVER A WEEK WHICH IS QUITE AN ACHIEVEMENT STOP IT ONLY NEEDS INSTRUCTIONS FROM YOU TO LIGHT ME UP AGAIN MUCH LOVE GERTRUDE LAWRENCE

And when an estate agent in Bermuda said that the house in Bermuda she was considering included a maid, a secretary and a chauffeur, she naturally sent a cable:

AIRMAIL PHOTOGRAPH OF CHAUFFEUR.

But it was her husband who was telegraphed the most. He got telegrams when she was flat-hunting:

FLAT-HUNTING AND STILL ADORINGLY YOURS.

And when the sun came out:

SUCH A GLORIOUS DAY AND I HAVE A MATINEE BUT I WANT YOU TO GO TO THE BEACH AND GET PLENTY OF SUN.

And on Valentine's Day:

AHOY THERE SAILOR ON THIS DAY MANY VOWS MAY COME YOUR WAY BUT SHOULD YOU TO OTHERS STOOP I STILL WOULD LOVE YOU CAUSE YOU'RE MY OLD POOP REMEMBER ME I'M THAT GAL YOU MARRIED.

And, of course, when she was coming home:

SPIT ON THE BRASS. CLEAR THE DECKS. GET THAT WOMAN OUT OF THE HOUSE. LEAVING THE SHOW IN ONE MONTH AND COMING HOME. MRS A

THE SHOW MUST GO ON

The theatre depends on telegrams; it couldn't get along without them. How could the curtain rise without telegrams like these?

Burgess Meredith to Lauren Bacall, who was starting her career with a small part at the Playhouse Theatre, Wilmington:

YOU MAY AS WELL START BEING A STAR IN WILMINGTON AS ANYWHERE. SO BE GOOD TONIGHT.

Peter Sellers to Spike Milligan on the opening of *Treasure Island* at the Mermaid Theatre:

LOOK HERE YOU NAUGHTY MAN WHAT'S GOING ON OVER THERE. I WAS
LOOKING THROUGH ME OLD PHOTOGRAPHS AND I SAW THAT YOU ARE DUE
TO DEPICT THE CHARACTER OF BEN GUNN AT TREASURE ISLAND ON
MERMAIDS. I ONCE HAD A RELATIVE WHO LIVED ON THE ISLAND BY
NAME OF MERVYN BLOOKNOK A POOVE BUT NOBUDY IS PERFECT AS YOU
WELL KNOW ANYWAY HE FELT NO PAIN. I HOPE YOU HAVE A GRAND
OPENING TONIGHT AH THAT'S BETTER. YOUR OLD FRIEND AND
COMMANDING OFFICER DENNIS BLOODNOK OF THE AMERICAS

Spike Milligan to Peter Sellers:

DEAR MAJOR BLOODNOK THERE MUST BE SOME MISTAKE STOP BEN GUNN IS
BEING PLAYED BY A FINE THIN PARISIAN THESPIAN ONE COMTE MORIARTY
WHO IS ESPECIALLY STARVED FOR THE PART SIGNED GRYTPYPE-THYNNE

Donald Wolfit to James Agate:

THANK YOU INDEED FOR YOUR MAGNIFICENT AND GENEROUS REVIEW OF MY
WORK STOP MAY I CONTINUE TO DESERVE IT OF YOU AND THE PUBLIC
STOP GARRICK IS MY YARD-STICK HE HAD VERSATILITY AND A ROUND
FACE TOO STOP WARMEST REGARDS.

George S. Kaufman to the actor Billy Gaxton during a performance of *Of Thee I Sing*:

WATCHING YOUR PERFORMANCE FROM LAST ROW. WISH YOU WERE HERE.

Alexander Woollcott to George S. Kaufman on his fifth wedding anniversary:

I HAVE BEEN LOOKING ROUND FOR AN APPROPRIATE WOODEN GIFT AND AM
PLEASED HEREBY TO PRESENT YOU WITH ELSIE FERGUSON'S PERFORMANCE
IN HER NEW PLAY.

When *Scènes de Ballet* was having its first performances in 1944, Anton Dolin sent a cable to Stravinsky:

BALLET GREAT SUCCESS STOP... CAN THE PAS DE DEUX BE ORCHESTRATED WITH THE STRINGS CARRYING THE MELODY THIS IS MOST IMPORTANT TO INSURE GREATER SUCCESS.

Stravinsky replied:

SATISFIED GREAT SUCCESS.

George Kaufman cabled his father while working as stage manager for a stock company in Troy, New York:

LAST SUPPER AND ORIGINAL CAST COULDN'T DRAW IN THIS HOUSE.

To Mrs Patrick Campbell in 1916:

DOCTOR WILL CUT OFF MY LEG NEXT MONDAY. AM VERY HAPPY. KISSES ALL MY HEART. SARAH BERNHARDT

Noël Coward, Rome, to Cole Lesley:
AM BACK FROM ISTANBUL WHERE I WAS KNOWN AS ENGLISH DELIGHT.

Noël Coward to Jack Wilson, after a bid from a New York radio station for the character Elvira in *Blithe Spirit*. They wanted it for a soap opera with Janet Gaynor:
IN NO CIRCUMSTANCES WHATSOEVER STOP SUGGEST THEY GET SHAW'S PERMISSION TO USE SAINT JOAN.

Noël Coward to his business manager, Jack Wilson:
VERY SORRY FIND MY ENGAGEMENTS WILL NOT PERMIT ME APPEAR UNDER YOUR BANNER IN AMERICA UNLESS I GET FURTHER 58 PER CENT OF THE GROSS FOR ARDUOUS TASK RESTRAINING MISS LAWRENCE FROM BEING GROCK, BEATRICE, THEDA BARA, MARY PICKFORD AND BERT LAHR ALL AT ONCE.

Noël Coward to Jack Wilson after Hollywood interest in *Blithe Spirit:*

ALL MY PLAYS EXCEPTING CAVALCADE HAVE BEEN VULGARISED DISTORTED
AND RUINED BY MOVIE MINDS AM NOW MIDDLE-AGED AND PRESTIGE AND
QUALITY OF MY WORK ARE MY ONLY ASSETS FOR THE FUTURE THEREFORE
HAVE DECIDED HENCEFORWARD NEVER TO SELL FILM RIGHTS UNLESS I
HAVE ABSOLUTE CONTROL OF SCRIPT DIALOGUE CAST TREATMENT DIRECTOR
CAMERAMAN CUTTER AND PUBLICITY CONVINCED PRESENT UNAVOIDABLE
LOSS IS FUTURE INEVITABLE GAIN.

DEADLINES

The artist Frederic Remington was sent to Cuba to make sketches of the war with Spain for the *New York Journal.* He found there was no war with Spain, so he sent the proprietor a telegram:

W.R. Hearst, *New York Journal,* March, 1898:

EVERYTHING IS QUIET. THERE IS NO TROUBLE HERE. THERE WILL BE NO WAR. I WISH TO RETURN. REMINGTON

William Randolph Hearst's celebrated cable thundered back.

Remington, Havana:

PLEASE REMAIN. YOU FURNISH THE PICTURES AND I'LL FURNISH THE WAR. W.R. HEARST

Arthur Brisbane was Hearst's golden-haired boy for a time, as well as his number one writer and main ideas man. Here is one of Brisbane's ideas, cabled urgently to the editor of the *New York Mirror:*

PERHAPS LOVE AND MARRIAGE PAGE NEEDS A DISCUSSION. IS MAN OR WOMAN MORE INTENSELY AFFECTIONATE? KEEP AWAY FROM ANYTHING DEALING TOO CLOSELY WITH SEX. FIND OUT WHETHER IMPULSE TOWARDS OTHER SEX AND TOWARD MARRIAGE AND CHILDREN IS STRONGER IN WOMEN OR IN MEN. I THINK IT TEN TIMES STRONGER IN WOMEN, MORE INSATIABLE FOR BIOLOGICAL REASONS. GET IMPORTANT PERSON, PREFERABLY CLERGYMAN, TO SAY THAT. PUT QUESTION TO WELL-KNOWN MEN AND WOMEN, ACTORS AND ACTRESSES, MOTION-PICTURE PEOPLE. PERHAPS SOME MOVIE LADY, DIVORCED SEVERAL TIMES, COULD BE CONSIDERED AN AUTHORITY. PERHAPS A BETTER AUTHORITY WOULD BE SOMEONE WHO MARRIED AND STAYED MARRIED. KEEP THIS ON HIGH PLANE. USE PICTURES OF THOSE INTERVIEWED BUT FOR GOD'S SAKE DON'T USE PHOTOGRAPHS OF HORRIBLE LOOKING MEN LIKE REV. DR. CADMAN OR THE LONG-NOSED MR. DURANTE.

But golden-headed boys all must like chimney sweepers come to dust; not long afterwards Brisbane got this crushing telegram from Hearst:

DEAR ARTHUR, YOU ARE NOW GETTING OUT THE WORST NEWSPAPER IN THE UNITED STATES.

Mr Shovelton of the *Manchester Guardian* would not, one feels, have cared for this sort of thing. But he, too, achieved immortality with a telegram.

Neville Cardus knew Shovelton and described him as a portly and venerable man. One day this portly and venerable man was alone in the office when news came through of a railway accident in the north. Mr Shovelton knew his duty. He left a note for the News Editor, picked up his black portmanteau and set off for the station.

All next day there was no news from Shovelton. The early editions of Monday morning's papers arrived and they all had the story but still nothing from Shovelton.

Then, with the News Editor in despair, a telegram arrived. The News Editor opened it. It read:

ARRIVED SAFELY.   SNOWING HARD.

Quentin Reynolds, a great American reporter, was working on the Lindbergh baby kidnapping story and sent his office a story about Old Lem who had seen a mystery car on the night of the crime. Then he discovered that Old Lem was the town drunk.

At the Western Union office a cable from his paper was waiting:

FINE STORY ABOUT LEM THE TRAPPER.   IS IT EXCLUSIVE?   LET ME KNOW SOONEST.

Soonest he let the office know:

STORY IS NOT ONLY ONE HUNDRED PER CENT EXCLUSIVE BUT ONE HUNDRED PER CENT PHONY.

In 1940 Reynolds was having trouble with the French. So he asked if he could cable his uncle in America and sent the following message to the White House:

DEAR UNCLE FRANKLIN, AM HAVING DIFFICULTY GETTING ACCREDITED TO THE FRENCH ARMY.   TIME IS IMPORTANT.   WOULD YOU PHONE OR CABLE PREMIER REYNAUD AND ASK HIM TO HURRY THINGS UP?   IT WAS GRAND OF YOU TO PHONE ME LAST NIGHT.   PLEASE GIVE MY LOVE TO AUNT ELEANOR.

He got accredited.

Foreign Editors like to hear from their far-flung reporters from time to time. Hence this celebrated exchange:

WHY UNNEWS?

UNNEWS GOOD NEWS.

UNNEWS UNJOB.

They also tend to wish they wouldn't spend quite so much:
    To William Forrest, Cape Town, from Accounts Department, *News Chronicle:*

SENT $400. PLEASE ACCOUNT.

To Accounts Department, *News Chronicle*, from William Forrest, Cape Town:

RECEIVED $400. SPENT $400. REGARDS. FORREST

News Editors can be fierce. United Press and the Press Association shared the same correspondent in a small American town which was suddenly engulfed by a monstrous flood.

The correspondent, coping with his first big story in years, was putting copy over to AP while UP kept pressing him for more. Exasperated, he sent UP an unwise message:

`BE WITH YOU IN A MINUTE.  OPERATOR HAS ONLY ONE PAIR OF HANDS.`

UP immediately wired back:

`FIRE THE CRIPPLED BASTARD.`

Features Editors, too, can speak their minds.

Ballet writer Richard Buckle received this cable from J.W. Lambert of the *Sunday Times* in London while he was on tour in Australia:

```
PERSONAL TOUCH WELCOME BUT MOST OF MATERIAL SO FAR SENT IS TOTALLY
UNUSABLE STOP WE NEED YOUR REACTIONS TO AUSTRALIA AUSTRALIANS AND
THE ARTS NOT TO A HANDFUL OF PEOPLE WHO SHOULD ONLY BE
INCIDENTAL STOP ALSO ON NO ACCOUNT CHARGE A PENNY OF ANY MONEY
SPENT ON OTHER INDIVIDUALS THEIR TRAVELS AND LIVING EXPENSES TO
SUNDAY TIMES STOP REGRET DISOBLIGING TONE BUT I AM TOTALLY
DISMAYED JACK
```

Buckle replied:

```
NOT ALTOGETHER SURPRISED YOUR REACTION IN VIEW ETERNAL POLICY
SUNDAY TIMES REDUCING ME GENERAL LEVEL MEDIOCRITY DARLING
RAYMOND AND DESMOND ALWAYS EXCEPTED ALSO SPORTS PAGE FROM WHICH
YOU HAVE A LOT TO LEARN WOULD NOT DREAM CHARGE YOU PENNY ARTISTS
EXPENSES KNOWING INGRAINED MIDDLECLASS LOATHING OF ART STOP IF
ONE SINGLE WORD CUT OR CHANGED OR MISPRINTED I RESIGN AND RETIRE
HALF PAY IF YOU CAN CALL IT PAY AS`ARRANGED EVANS ENORMOUS
RELIEF AND ECONOMY TO ME THOMSONS LOSS THE WORLDS GAIN LOVE
BUCKLE
```

The newspaper printed a cut version of Buckle's script and he resigned.

Arthur Cook, covering the 1951 Iranian crisis, got a notable scoop. Mossadegh, who had nationalised the oil, banished the Shah, burst into frequent tears and alarmed everyone, had been assassinated.

Cook's paper splashed the sensational story across its front page. But alack the day, Mossadegh turned up as large as life. He had not been assassinated at all.

There was a telegram for Mr Cook from his Foreign Editor:

EITHER YOU OR MOSSADEGH DIES TONIGHT.

A foreign correspondent must know no fear. Observe Mr W. Buchanan Taylor, London correspondent of *Variety,* bursting into the suite occupied by the French star Gaby Deslys and her new young escort, Harry Pilcer.

What *Variety* and indeed the world wished to know, said Mr Taylor, was whether they were married? Reclining in her négligé, Madame Deslys said no they weren't and Taylor sent his cable:

GABY AND PILCER SAY NOT MARRIED. THINK THEY SHOULD BE.

Still, it is usually the foreign correspondent who has the last word.

When Evelyn Waugh was covering the Abyssinian war, a story broke about a hospital at Adowa being bombed and an American nurse killed. Neither Waugh nor anyone else on the spot could identify the hospital but cables were arriving from London and New York:

REQUIRE EARLIEST NAME LIFE STORY PHOTOGRAPH AMERICAN NURSE
UPBLOWN ADOWA.

Waugh replied:

NURSE UNUPBLOWN

'...and after a few days,' Waugh wrote in *Waugh in Abyssinia,* 'she disappeared from the news.'

Sometimes editors get telegrams themselves.

In May 1932 the sensational story of the moment was that Nancy Cunard had chased Paul Robeson across the Atlantic and was staying with him at a Harlem hotel.

On 2 May she sent this wire to the New York *Daily Mirror:*

RACKET MY DEAR SIR, PURE RACKET, HEIRESS AND ROBESON STUFF. IMMEDIATELY CORRECT THESE. CALL MONDAY ONE O'CLOCK GIVE YOU TRUE STATEMENT. NANCY CUNARD. PUBLISH THIS.

They didn't. They *did* publish Robeson's denial though.

Journalists, as we all know, like to get things right. A magazine editor cabled Cary Grant's agent:

HOW OLD CARY GRANT?

The answer, from Mr Grant himself, is now famous:

OLD CARY GRANT FINE. HOW YOU?

Proprietors get telegrams too.

To Lord Northcliffe, from his mother:

ALFRED I CANNOT MAKE UP MY MIND WHICH OF YOUR TWO PRINCIPAL PAPERS IS THE MORE VULGAR THIS MORNING.

Mind you, foreign telegrams can be confusing.

In June 1914 the Reuter's sports desk in London, awaiting the results of the 2.30 at Longchamps, got a telegram from its Paris office:

ARCHEDUC ASSASSINE SARAJEVO.

'Not an English horse in the first three,' said the Chief Sub, and spiked it.

LITERARY LINES

Four telegrams played a key role in the early stages of Ernest Hemingway's literary career.

His first American book, the collection of short stories *In Our Time,* had been published by Boni and Liveright. Hemingway then sent them *The Torrents of Spring,* a satire he had written in a week during a break from working on his first novel, *The Sun Also Rises.*

Then a cable arrived from Boni and Liveright:

REJECTING TORRENTS OF SPRING PATIENTLY AWAITING MANUSCRIPT SUN ALSO RISES WRITING FULLY.

F. Scott Fitzgerald, who enormously admired Hemingway's work, at once cabled Scribner's, his own publishers:

YOU CAN GET HEMINGWAYS FINISHED NOVEL PROVIDED YOU PUBLISH UNPROMISING SATIRE HARCOURT HAS MADE DEFINITE OFFER WIRE IMMEDIATELY WITHOUT QUALIFICATIONS.

Scribner's wired the same day:

PUBLISH NOVEL AT FIFTEEN PER CENT AND ADVANCE IF DESIRED ALSO
SATIRE UNLESS OBJECTIONABLE OTHER THAN FINANCIALLY.

And three days later:

CONFIDENCE ABSOLUTE KEEN TO PUBLISH.

That was enough. Scribner's had acquired one of the world's great novelists for its list. They got *The Sun Also Rises* and all the books that followed.

Oscar Wilde to the citizens of Griggsville, Kansas, who had invited him to give a lecture. They were, they said, most eager to learn about aesthetics. Wilde sent them a wire:

BEGIN BY CHANGING THE NAME OF YOUR TOWN.

Publishers often need to say no thank you.
     To Michael Joseph from an author:

MUST HAVE IMMEDIATE DECISION AS HAVE OTHER IRONS IN FIRE.

From Michael Joseph to author:

SUGGEST YOU EXTRACT IRONS AND INSERT TYPESCRIPT.

So do authors:

E.B. White to Henry Canby:

VERY GRATEFUL FOR YOUR INVITATION BUT FEEL IT IS TOO EARLY IN LIFE TO JOIN AN INSTITUTE OF LETTERS AS IN MY PRESENT CONDITION I CAN BARELY KEEP UP WITH LETTERS THEMSELVES. THIS IS IN KEEPING WITH MY DISINCLINATION TO BELONG TO CLUBS AND SOCIETIES EVEN INCLUDING THOSE FOR WHICH I HAVE THE HIGHEST REGARD. WITH MANY THANKS, E.B. WHITE

Groucho Marx to a company that wanted to publish his letters:

YOUR LETTER RECEIVED AND PROMPTLY BURNED. I PREFER NOT TO HAVE STRANGERS PRYING INTO MY MAIL. WOULD DISCUSS THIS IN DETAIL BUT MY SECRETARY HAS A DATE IN FIVE MINUTES — WITH ME.

James Agate put the *Radio Times* in its place:

I SEE YOU ANNOUNCE PHYLLIS NEILSON-TERRY AND LESLIE BANKS IN
MACBETH. DID YOU EVER SEE ELLEN TERRY AND HENRY IRVING IN
HAMLET? OR PERHAPS YOU ONLY SAW THEM IN JULIET AND ROMEO?

Charles Osborne's biography of W.H. Auden provoked this huffy response from a
reader:

    To the Director, Eyre Methuen:

HAVING WORKED WITH AUDEN AND AS PARTICIPATOR AND LATER CO
ARTISTIC DIRECTOR OF GROUP THEATRE TAKE ABSOLUTE EXCEPTION TO
CHARLES OSBORNE MALIGNING FALSELY MY COLLEAGUE THE LATE RUPERT
DOONE STOP IT IS INEXCUSABLE AND SHALL BE VIGOROUSLY PURSUED.
VERA RUSSELL

Osborne replied:

THANK YOU FOR TELEGRAM TO MY PUBLISHER OFFERING VIGOROUSLY TO
PUBLICISE MY AUDEN BOOK STOP GRATEFULLY ACCEPT YOUR OFFER.

The novelist Norman Douglas skipped bail in 1916 when charges were pending over a case involving a young man. He did not return to the UK until 1941, when he wired a friend:

FEEL LIKE A BOY AGAIN.

Ring Lardner to a friend on holiday:

WHEN ARE YOU COMING BACK AND WHY?

And *Collier's Magazine* came in for the edge of F. Scott Fitzgerald's tongue when it hesitated to serialise *The Last Tycoon.*

To Maxwell Perkins:

I HAVEN'T SEEN A PIECE OF FICTION IN THERE FOR SEVERAL YEARS THAT WOULD SERVE THE PURPOSE OF A SEARS ROEBUCK CATALOGUE.

Angus Wilson, on holiday in Sicily, sent telegrams to three of his friends. To one, a virologist, he sent:

PLISS VIRE US SOONEST.

And to another, who had never been to Sicily and was not about to visit, he sent:

YOUR LECTURE WOMEN'S CLUB AGRIGENTO CANCELLED.

'I can't remember the third,' he says. 'I enjoyed sending them but nobody laughed but me.'

Punch reported that Oscar Wilde and James McNeill Whistler had been heard discussing Sarah Bernhardt. Wilde at once telegraphed Whistler:

PUNCH TOO RIDICULOUS. WHEN YOU AND I ARE TOGETHER WE NEVER TALK ABOUT ANYTHING BUT OURSELVES.

Whistler replied:

NO, NO, OSCAR, YOU FORGET. WHEN YOU AND I ARE TOGETHER WE NEVER TALK ABOUT ANYTHING EXCEPT ME.

To which Wilde replied:

IT IS TRUE WE WERE TALKING ABOUT YOU. BUT I WAS THINKING OF MYSELF.

Director Mervyn le Roy to Jack Warner of Warner Brothers:
PLEASE READ ANTHONY ADVERSE. WOULD MAKE GREAT PICTURE FOR US.

Jack Warner to Mervyn le Roy:
READ IT? I CAN'T EVEN LIFT IT.

The last thing that T.E. Lawrence (alias J. H. Ross or T. E. Shaw) did was to send a telegram:
LUNCH TUESDAY WET FINE COTTAGE ONE MILE NORTH BOVINGTON CAMP.
SHAW
He sent this to Henry Williamson at Bovington Camp on 13 May 1935. Then he climbed onto his Brough motorcycle and sped off back to Clouds Hill and the crash that killed him.

BAD NEWS AND CALCULATED INSULTS

The telegram has broken enough bad news in its day, God knows. There cannot be many families who have not, at some time, had a telegram like:

Bertie to Queen Victoria, 14 January 1892:

OUR DARLING EDDY HAS BEEN TAKEN FROM US. WE ARE BROKEN HEARTED.

And in two world wars, whenever a man was killed or wounded or reported missing it was usually a telegram that let his family know. Small wonder that many hearts still miss a beat when a telegram arrives.

But on sad occasions telegrams can be consoling.

   Alexander Woollcott to the distinguished American actor Otis Skinner on the death of his wife Maud:

YOU LUCKY BASTARD TO HAVE HAD ALL THOSE YEARS WITH THAT
EXQUISITE PERSON.

And they can make excuses.

   Jack Dempsey (after losing the world heavyweight championship to Gene Tunney) to John Barrymore:

DEAR JACK. I FORGOT TO DUCK.

And they can say goodbye.

   Lois Morgan to Scott and Zelda Fitzgerald when they were leaving Hollywood in 1927:

BOOTLEGGERS GONE OUT OF BUSINESS COTTON CLUB CLOSED ALL FLAGS AT
HALF MAST... BOTTLES OF LOVE TO YOU BOTH.

They can say 'No thank you'.

Peter Arno to Irving Penn, after an invitation to appear in a *New Yorker* group photograph for *Vogue:*

I CAN'T STAND CROWDS.

They can ask for sympathy.

Noël Coward, Florence, to Cole Lesley:

HAVE MOVED HOTEL EXCELSIOR COUGHING MYSELF INTO A FIRENZE.

And they can relay insults, complaints and home-truths for any occasion.

David Niven, trapped on the set of the disastrous *Bonnie Prince Charlie*, to Sam Goldwyn:

I HAVE NOW WORKED EVERY DAY FOR FIVE MONTHS ON THIS PICTURE AND NOBODY CAN TELL ME HOW THE STORY ENDS STOP ADVISE.

Frankie Howerd to the management during the provincial tour of *Mr Venus:*
HAVE ANY OF YOU ACTUALLY SEEN IT?
They wanted to bring it into London — and did.

Lord Alfred Douglas to his father, the Marquess of Queensberry:
WHAT A FUNNY LITTLE MAN YOU ARE.
This 'foolish and vulgar telegram', wrote Wilde to Douglas, 'conditioned the whole of your subsequent relations with your father and consequently the whole of my life'.

Lord Queensberry mid-trial to his daughter-in-law, 20 May 1895:
MUST CONGRATULATE ON VERDICT. CANNOT ON PERCY'S APPEARANCE, LOOKED LIKE A DUG UP CORPSE. FEAR TOO MUCH MADNESS OF KISSING. TAYLOR GUILTY. WILDE'S TURN TOMORROW. QUEENSBERRY

Florenz Ziegfeld to Eddie Cantor:

MERRY CHRISTMAS TO YOU AND YOURS. MAY WE REMAIN TOGETHER AS
LONG AS WE BOTH REMAIN IN SHOW BUSINESS ALTHOUGH PROFITS ON
'KIDS BOOTS' HAVE BEEN FAR LESS THAN ON 'SALLY'.

Puccini sent *panettone,* a Milanese style of cake, to his friends at Christmas. One
year he fell out with Toscanini.
    To Toscanini:

PANETTONE SENT BY MISTAKE. PUCCINI

To Puccini:

PANETTONE EATEN BY MISTAKE. TOSCANINI

When Khrushchev visited Oxford in 1956 he made disparaging remarks about Epstein's Lazarus in New College chapel. The warden of New College received this telegram:

TELL YOUR GUEST TO KEEP OFF ART CRITICISM WHICH HE DOES NOT UNDERSTAND AND STICK TO HIS OWN BUSINESS WHICH IS MURDER.
EPSTEIN

Sir Arthur Conan Doyle claimed that he once sent identical telegrams to twelve distinguished men. They read:

ALL IS DISCOVERED. FLY AT ONCE.

The twelve, he said, all left the country within twenty-four hours.

ANOTHER DAY, ANOTHER DOLLAR

Telegrams permit you to offer your services or seek help, financial or otherwise...

To Mr James Forrestal, Under Secretary of the Navy, on America's entry into the Second World War:

I AM FORTY-NINE BUT IN GOOD HEALTH, HAVE OWNED THREE YACHTS AND AM EXPERIENCED IN THEIR CARE AND MAINTENANCE. IF NAVY CAN USE ME IN ANY CAPACITY PLEASE ADVISE. REGARDS PAUL GETTY

Billy Milton, the entertainer, to Robert Nesbitt and Joan Davis, producing a show at the Palladium:

I'M THE ONLY JUVENILE LEFT IN THE BUSINESS WHO CAN GET HIS TEETH INTO THE PART AND NOT LEAVE THEM THERE.

Lynn Fontanne to Robert Sherwood after reading his play *There Shall Be No Night:*
THIS HALF IS COMING BACK TO REHEARSE.

To Robert Sherwood from Miss Fontanne's husband, Alfred Lunt, after *he* had read it:
THE OTHER HALF IS COMING TOO.

The directors of the Norwich Festival once asked the great soprano Adelina Patti 'Why such a fee at a music festival?' She replied by telegram:
I AM A MUSIC FESTIVAL.

Will Rogers, American humourist and actor, to the President of the United States:

```
PLEASE SEND MONEY, UNEXPECTED DIPLOMATIC RELATIONS HAVE SUDDENLY
ARISEN HERE WHICH NO ONE COULD FORESEE.  PLEASE RUSH AS FRENCH
TAXI DRIVER IS WAITING.  WILLROG
```

The Queen Mother's father inherited £10 million but was rather stingy with the pocket money. Hence the telegram from the youngest contributor to this collection.
    Lady Elizabeth Bowes-Lyon, aged seven, to the 14th Earl of Strathmore:

```
SOS LSD RSVP ELIZABETH
```

Donald Wolfit, then a young schoolmaster, had the same message for *his* father — though he was more specific:

```
HAVE JOINED CHARLES DORAN'S SHAKESPEARE COMPANY.  PLEASE SEND
£30.
```

He got it.

When Frank Sinatra asked Noël Coward to state his terms for a guest appearance on his television show Coward spelled them out:

ONE HUNDRED THOUSAND DOLLARS PLUS MY EXPENSES AND THE RETURN AIR FARE FROM GENEVA.

He didn't get it.

Carl Laemmle Jnr to his father, the founder of Universal Pictures:

PLEASE WIRE MORE MONEY AM TALKING TO FRENCH COUNT RE MOVIE.

His father replied:

NO MONEY TILL YOU LEARN TO SPELL.

Zelda (just released from hospital after her breakdown) to Scott Fitzgerald:

I WONT BE ABLE TO STICK THIS OUT. WILL YOU WIRE MONEY
IMMEDIATELY THAT I MAY RETURN FRIDAY TO ASHVILLE (the hospital).
WILL SEE SCOTTY (their daughter) THERE. DEVOTEDLY REGRETFULLY
GRATEFULLY ZELDA

And later that afternoon:

DISREGARD TELEGRAM AM FINE AGAIN. HAPPY TO SEE SCOTTY.
DEVOTEDLY. ZELDA

They can offer you a job.
    Herman Mankiewicz to Ben Hecht, 1925:

WILL YOU ACCEPT THREE HUNDRED PER WEEK TO WORK FOR PARAMOUNT
PICTURES. ALL EXPENSES PAID. THE THREE HUNDRED IS PEANUTS.
MILLIONS ARE TO BE GRABBED OUT HERE AND YOUR ONLY COMPETITION IS
IDIOTS. DON'T LET THIS GET AROUND.

After the Russian revolution Lewis J. Selznick sent this telegram to the Tsar:

WHEN I WAS A BOY IN RUSSIA YOUR POLICE TREATED MY PEOPLE VERY BADLY. HOWEVER NO HARD FEELINGS. HEAR YOU ARE NOW OUT OF WORK. IF YOU WILL COME TO NEW YORK CAN GIVE YOU FINE POSITION ACTING IN PICTURES. SALARY NO OBJECT. REPLY MY EXPENSE. REGARDS YOU AND FAMILY.

He received no reply.

Telegrams also permit you to do some chatting up...
George S. Kaufman to prospective dinner date:

MAGNIFICENT CAR WILL BE AT YOUR DOOR TOMORROW NIGHT SIX THIRTY. DON'T BE AFRAID OF WHITE SLAVERY, GET RIGHT IN.

Alexander Woollcott to Margalo Gillmore:

BEFORE YOU SIGN UP WITH WEE AND LEVENTHAL GEORGE AND I HAVE WRITTEN A PART FOR YOU. TWELVE CHANGES OF CLOTHES.

Telegrams can give you courage to face the terrors ahead:

To American actress Elaine Stritch from BBC interviewer Russell Harty when she took over his radio show *Midweek:*

LOOKING FORWARD TO LYING IN BED LISTENING. ANYWAY. IF YOU GET
STUCK, KEEP SAYING ANYWAY. ANYWAY. LOVE RUSSELL

Awaiting Evelyn Waugh on taking up employment as a schoolmaster at a prep school, from Hugh Lygon and John Sutro:

ON, EVELYN, ON.

And they can give you the old heave-ho!

To a famous movie star travelling incognito across America with her lover, also incognito:

TELL NIVEN CALL GOLDWYN IMMEDIATELY JOCK

TELL NIVEN CALL ME TONIGHT WITHOUT FAIL GOLDWYN

ASK NIVEN WHAT HE THINKS HE'S DOING HAVE HIM CALL TONIGHT OR
ELSE GOLDWYN

TELL NIVEN HE'S FIRED GOLDWYN

Or a declaration of love:

DEAR MISS MAYER: YOUR MANUSCRIPT IS THE MOST MAGNIFICENT I HAVE
EVER RECEIVED. CANNOT COMMENT TOO HIGHLY ON YOUR HUMOUR,
ORIGINALITY, SINCERITY AND SHEER WRITING ABILITY. BECAUSE OF
THE FINE PROMISE SHOWN BY EVERYTHING YOU HAVE DONE TO DATE YOU
MAY CONSIDER YOURSELF ENGAGED ON YOUR OWN TERMS. D.O. SELZNICK

Miss Mayer was Louis B. Mayer's daughter; David O. Selznick was a rising young
director at Paramount. The manuscript was a letter from Miss Mayer to Mr Selznick.
They married soon afterwards.

MAIL ~ ORDER

Then there is the mail-order telegram.

This is John Barrymore's telegraphed order for his aviary:

ONE BLUE-CROWNED MOTMOT, TWO SMALL TOUCANS. PLEASE DO NOT CLIP
WINGS ANY MORE, AS WISH THEM TO FLY IF POSSIBLE. TWO
OROPENDULARS, ONE CRIMSON-BACK TANAGER, ONE BLUE TANAGER. THREE
PAIRS HONEY-CREEPERS, AND ONE OR TWO TROGONS. PLEASE TELEGRAPH
ME NAME OF BOAT AND DATE ARRIVAL SAN PEDRO WHEN BIRDS ARE
SHIPPED.

Robert L. (Believe-It-Or-Not) Ripley would have considered such an order very mundane. Here are two telegraphed orders of his. (He was restocking his odditorium.):

CAN USE MAN BED NAILS UPSIDEDOWN MAN SUNGAZER UPARM MAN HUGE EARRING WOMAN HORNED MAN STOP SUGGEST YOU COMMUNICATE WITH BOMBAY REFERENCE NAILSITTER KNIFEJUGGLER AND FOOD CONTROLLER STOP WANT ALL THESE IMMEDIATELY SAIL NEXT BOAT.

And:

CABLING YOU THREE HUNDRED RUPEES FOR EMBARKATION ALSO FIFTY DOLLARS EXPENSES TO OBTAIN HORNED MAN STOP CANNOT USE LONGNECK GIRLS.

And Noël Coward's telegraphed order was exotic enough for the time being. (He was stocking his new revue, *Set to Music.*)
    To Jack Wilson, New York:

SUGGEST YOU ENGAGE EIGHT REALLY BEAUTIFUL SHOWGIRLS MORE OR LESS SAME HEIGHT NO PARTICULAR TALENT REQUIRED.

AWAY FROM IT ALL

Robert Benchley, Venice, to *The New Yorker:*
STREETS FULL OF WATER. PLEASE ADVISE.

Indian stationmaster to Collector:
TIGER ON PLATFORM STOP STAFF FRIGHTENED STOP PRAY ATTEND.

And, in another part of the empire...
    District Officer to Cairo:
POST SURROUNDED BY LIONS AND TIGERS.

Cairo to District Officer:
THERE ARE NO TIGERS IN AFRICA.

District Officer to Cairo:
DELETE TIGERS.

If all else fails there is the telegram to yourself. AUNT ILL COME AT ONCE has salvaged many a lost weekend.

Beverley Nichols tried this when staying with Somerset Maugham at his villa in Cap d'Antibes. He was not enjoying it so sent a cable to his agent in London:

RAY SAVAGE LONDON SITUATION HERE QUITE IMPOSSIBLE STOP PLEASE CABLE SAYING COMPLICATIONS ABOUT MY PLAY DEMAND MY IMMEDIATE PRESENCE LONDON LOVE BEVERLEY

The reply came that afternoon:

BEVERLEY NICHOLS CARE OF MAUGHAM VILLA MAURESQUE CAP D'ANTIBES FRANCE ALPES MARITIMES REGRET INFORM YOU SERIOUS TROUBLE ABOUT CASTING PLAY STOP CANNOT DEAL WITH THIS ALONE AS AUTHORS DECISION VITAL STOP HATE INTERRUPTING YOUR HOLIDAY BUT SO MUCH AT STAKE THAT FEEL YOU SHOULD RETURN IMMEDIATELY LOVE RAYMOND

Nichols, telegram in hand, broke the news to Maugham who was clearly not deceived. When Maugham was angry he stuttered, and he stuttered now.

'I s-s-see,' he said. 'At l-l-least I hope you feel able to s-s-stay to d-d-dinner,' and, turning his back, made for the dining room.

Or there is the candid approach, as from Monsieur de Guermantes in Proust's *Le Temps Retrouvé*:

IMPOSSIBLE TO COME. LIE FOLLOWS.

G.K. Chesterton's legendary telegram to his wife has been allotted to just about every railway station in England.
   It really read:

AM IN MARKET HARBOROUGH. WHERE OUGHT I TO BE?

Mrs Chesterton wired back:

HOME.

As she explained to Chesterton's biographer, Maisie Ward, it was easier to get him home and start him off again. That day's engagements were hopelessly lost anyway.

Lieutenant David Niven, Palm Beach, to Colonel Alec Telfer-Smollett, DSO MC:
DEAR COLONEL MAGNIFICENT OPPORTUNITY BIG GAME HUNTING WHALE
FISHING FLORIDA REQUEST ONE WEEK EXTENDED LEAVE.

Colonel Alec Telfer-Smollett, Dover, to Lieutenant David Niven:
NO WHALES OR BIG GAME WITHIN A THOUSAND MILES STOP TAKE TWO
SMOLLET

TIDINGS OF COMFORT AND JOY

Telegrams are best at bringing good news. So hurrah for good news telegrams.
Here are some of them:

To the Earl of Carnarvon, 6 November 1922:

AT LAST HAVE MADE WONDERFUL DISCOVERY IN VALLEY STOP MAGNIFICENT
TOMB WITH SEALS INTACT STOP RECOVERED SAME FOR YOUR ARRIVAL
CONGRATULATIONS HOWARD CARTER

On 17 February 1923, Carter opened the sealed door of the tomb of Tutankhamen.

Lord Beaverbrook to movie mogul Jack Warner, who wished to know if it was safe to visit Europe in 1938:

PERFECTLY ALL RIGHT TO COME HERE. I DON'T THINK THERE WILL BE
ANY EUROPEAN WAR. BRITAIN WILL NOT BE INVOLVED OR FRANCE EITHER
IN MY OPINION WITH KINDEST REGARDS TO YOU AND ANN. BEAVERBROOK

The pre-arranged telegram to King George V and Queen Mary from their second son telling them that he had proposed and been accepted by Lady Elizabeth Bowes-Lyon read:

ALL RIGHT. BERTIE

To the architect Frank Lloyd Wright after the great Tokyo earthquake in 1923:

FOLLOWING WIRELESS RECEIVED FROM TOKIO TODAY HOTEL STANDS
UNDAMAGED AS MONUMENT OF YOUR GENIUS HUNDREDS OF HOMELESS
PROVIDED BY PERFECTLY MAINTAINED SERVICE CONGRATULATIONS SIGNED
OKURA IMPEHO

Cole Porter to Louis Shurr, Hollywood:

I AM SENDING TODAY SEVERAL COPIES OF A SONG FROM SHOW TITLED
QUOTE IT'S ALL RIGHT WITH ME UNQUOTE WHICH I WROTE ESPECIALLY
FOR YOU. PLEASE SCATTER IT AMONG YOUR DANCE ORCHESTRAS BUT
DON'T LET THEM PLAY IT TOO FAST AS YOU SHOULD CRY WHEN YOU SING
IT. LOVE COLE

Richard Tauber to Franz Lehár, after the American premiere of his operetta *The Land of Smiles* (or *Yours Is My Heart,* as it was called on Broadway in 1946):
MUSIC MADE FANTASTIC IMPRESSION STOP THEY LIKED ME TREMENDOUSLY.

Ernest Hemingway to Maxwell Perkins, announcing that *For Whom the Bell Tolls* was nearly ready:
BRIDGE ALL BLOWN UP AM ENDING LAST CHAPTER.

When John Barrymore married Dolores Costello, he promised her mother he would cable every day of their honeymoon cruise. Forty-three days later Mrs Costello at last got a wire:
DOLORES IS WONDERFUL.

Unnamed patient on holiday to unnamed psychiatrist:
HAVING WONDERFUL TIME. WHY?

F. Scott Fitzgerald, New York, to Zelda Sayre, February 1919:
I AM IN THE LAND OF AMBITION AND SUCCESS AND MY ONLY HOPE AND
FAITH IS THAT MY DARLING HEART WILL BE WITH ME SOON.

Norma Shearer to F. Scott Fitzgerald:
I THOUGHT YOU WERE ONE OF THE MOST AGREEABLE PERSONS AT OUR TEA.

CONGRATULATIONS AND JUBILATIONS

When it comes to congratulations, nothing can beat a telegram...

James McNeill Whistler to Oscar Wilde and Constance Lloyd on the occasion of their marriage at St James' Church, Paddington:
AM DETAINED. DON'T WAIT.

To Gertrude Lawrence on the occasion of her marriage to Richard S. Aldrich:
DEAR MRS A, HOORAY HOORAY
AT LAST YOU ARE DEFLOWERED.
ON THIS AS EVERY OTHER DAY
I LOVE YOU. NOEL COWARD

To Hollywood agent Leland Hayward on his elopement with his beautiful client Margaret Sullavan from Walter Wanger:

CONGRATULATIONS ON GETTING THE OTHER NINETY PER CENT.

To beautiful client Margaret Sullavan on her elopement with her agent Leland Hayward from Katharine Hepburn:

DEAR MAGGIE, YOU HAVE JUST MARRIED THE MOST WONDERFUL MAN IN THE WORLD. BLESSINGS, KATE

In her autobiography, *An Unfinished Woman*, Lillian Hellman writes with affection about her maiden aunt Jenny.

One day, says Miss Hellman, a young woman asked Aunt Jenny how she could avoid pregnancy.

'Have a glass of ice water right before the sacred act, and three sips during it,' replied Aunt Jenny.

Years later when Miss Hellman was about to marry, she wrote to her aunts with the news. They sent back a telegram:

FORGET ABOUT THE GLASS OF ICE WATER TIMES HAVE CHANGED.

Dorothy Parker to Robert Sherwood's wife Mary on the birth of her baby:
DEAR MARY, WE ALL KNEW YOU HAD IT IN YOU.

Eddie Cantor to actress Norma Shearer and producer Irving Thalberg on the birth of a son:
CONGRATULATIONS ON YOUR LATEST PRODUCTION STOP SURE IT WILL LOOK BETTER AFTER ITS BEEN CUT.

Other events, too, call for a pat on the back:

John C. Flinn (a sales executive) to Cecil B. de Mille, 23 September 1919:
HAVE JUST SEEN 'MALE AND FEMALE'. A THOUSAND CONGRATULATIONS. IT IS NOT ONLY THE FINEST PICTURE IN EVERY PARTICULAR OF LOVE STORY AND SPECTACLE THAT YOU HAVE EVER MADE IT IS THE FINEST PICTURE EVER PRODUCED.

To Katharine Cornell on receiving an honorary doctorate of letters from the University of Wisconsin, from Noel Coward:

```
DARLING DARLING DOCTOR KITTY
THOUGH QUITE REASONABLY PRETTY
THOUGH UNDOUBTEDLY A STAR, DEAR
PLEASE REMEMBER WHO YOU ARE, DEAR.
WHY, IN LIEU OF ALL YOUR BETTERS,
SHOULD YOU HAVE DISTINGUISHED LETTERS?
THIS COMES FROM THE JEALOUS SOEL
OF YOUR SOMEDAY DOCTOR NOEL
```

W.H. Auden to E.M. Forster when he turned eighty:

```
DEAR MORGAN WISH I COULD BE WITH YOU IN MORE THAN SPIRIT STOP
MAY YOU LONG CONTINUE WHAT YOU ALREADY ARE STOP OLD FAMOUS LOVED
YET NOT A SACRED COW STOP LOVE AND GRATITUDE.
```

To a consultant at a large hospital in the north-east on his appointment as Honorary Physician to the Queen:

CONGRATULATIONS. GOD SAVE THE QUEEN.

Congratulations from the Queen, of course, always make the day. Not a day passes without someone somewhere in the British Commonwealth getting a telegram that reads:

THE QUEEN SENDS YOU WARM CONGRATULATIONS AND GOOD WISHES ON YOUR DIAMOND WEDDING DAY. PRIVATE SECRETARY

And any of her loyal citizens could receive the Queen's most famous telegram. All they have to do is to stay around long enough. This is what it says:

THE QUEEN IS MUCH INTERESTED TO HEAR THAT YOU ARE CELEBRATING YOUR HUNDREDTH BIRTHDAY AND SENDS YOU WARM CONGRATULATIONS AND GOOD WISHES. PRIVATE SECRETARY

STOP